SPEAKING
AS A
LEADER

SPEAKING

AS A

LEADER

HOW TO LEAD EVERY TIME YOU SPEAK

From Boardrooms to Meeting Rooms, From
Town Halls to Phone Calls

Judith Humphrey

John Wiley & Sons Canada, Ltd.

Library and Archives Canada Cataloguing in Publication
Humphrey, Judith, 1943–
  Speaking as a leader : how to lead every time you speak—from boardrooms to meeting rooms, from town halls to phone calls / Judith Humphrey.

Includes index.
Issued also in electronic formats.
ISBN 978-1-118-14101-4

  1. Communication in management. 2. Business communication.
3. Leadership. I. Title.

HD30.3.H86 2011   658.4'5   C2011-906155-4

E-ISBNs: 978-1-118-14755-9, 978-1-118-14756-6, 978-1-118-14757-3

Production Credits
Cover Concept: Ben Egnal
Cover Design: Adrian So
Composition: Thomson Digital
Printer: Friesens Printing Ltd.

Editorial Credits
Executive Editor: Karen Milner
Production Editor: Pauline Ricablanca

John Wiley & Sons Canada, Ltd.
6045 Freemont Blvd.
Mississauga, Ontario
L5R 4J3

Printed in Canada

1 2 3 4 5 FP 16 15 14 13 12

ENVIRONMENTAL BENEFITS STATEMENT

John Wiley & Sons Canada, Ltd. saved the following resources by printing the pages of this book on chlorine free paper made with 100% post-consumer waste.

TREES	WATER	ENERGY	SOLID WASTE	GREENHOUSE GASES
67	30,708	28	1,946	6,810
FULLY GROWN	GALLONS	MILLION BTUs	POUNDS	POUNDS

Environmental impact estimates were made using the Environmental Paper Network Paper Calculator. For more information visit www.papercalculator.org.

CONTENTS

CONTENTS

CONTENTS

PREFACE

This book has grown out of The Humphrey Group's privileged work with leaders in business, government, and not-for-profit organizations over the past 23 years. It's a book that will show you how to lead every time you speak, whether you are addressing a town hall, making a presentation, fielding challenging questions, or talking one-on-one with a colleague.

My interest in helping executives and managers communicate more effectively dates back to the 1980s and my years as a corporate speechwriter. I realized that most business executives would benefit from coaching, and saw an entrepreneurial opportunity.

My plans came together when I had lunch with an actor, Marshall Bell, who was then visiting Toronto. Marshall is a veteran actor. You've seen him if you're a movie buff. He's had roles in *Diggstown, Twins, Total Recall,* and many other films and television productions.

On a napkin we planned a new firm, one that combined his talents as an actor and coach with mine as a writer. Our first clients were top executives in the oil and banking industries, and together we taught them how to inspire their audiences. The Humphrey Group continues to draw upon the talents of a remarkable group of stage and screen actors.

Today The Humphrey Group, with offices in Toronto and Vancouver, coaches leaders around the globe. On any given day, our instructors might be teaching mine managers in Reno, executives in a retail firm in Mexico City, or leaders in Abu Dhabi. Our communication program for women—*Taking the Stage®*—has reached more than 100,000 female leaders around the world, including women in Tokyo, Hong Kong, London, and major centers across North America.

Readers of this book will gain the insights we in The Humphrey Group have acquired over nearly a quarter century. You will discover why our courses have met such a need and why companies and their leaders are inspired by what they learn from us. It's a work that goes far beyond the "tips" and "secrets" of speaking offered in many other books. Rather, on every page it emphasizes the need to speak as a leader. And it provides *one* model for all situations. That's why you'll find in every chapter examples from formal speech making, meeting presentations, and informal conversations.

The examples in this book are also drawn from various sources. Many chapter openings are from Lewis Carroll, author of *Alice's Adventures in Wonderland* and *Through the Looking-Glass*. While these are thought to be children's books, they have great wisdom beyond their supposed audience.

PREFACE

You will encounter famous speakers like Benazir Bhutto, Margaret Thatcher, Martin Luther King, Jr., Bill Clinton, Steve Jobs, GE's Jeffrey Immelt, and English physicist Stephen Hawking. You'll also find depictions of individuals The Humphrey Group has coached. We have always learned from our clients as they have learned from us. For the most part, I've changed the names of the individuals and their companies to safeguard their privacy. Linda Stromme, Principal at End Result Consulting, provided the "Story of Commitment."

I am indebted to the members of The Humphrey Group, a talented team of professionals with business and acting backgrounds. They have inspired me with their intelligence, superb coaching, and devotion to clients. All of them have contributed directly or indirectly to our methodology and the creation of this book. Nicky Guadagni provided much of the material for the chapter "Find Your Leader's Voice," and Linda Griffiths contributed to the chapters "Bring Your Script to Life" and "Suit the Action to the Word." Adam Bradley assisted with chapters throughout. Bart Egnal, Rob Borg-Olivier, Brenda Allen, Maggie Huculak, and Cynthia Ward read and commented thoughtfully on much of the text. Jodi Ann Smith encouraged me to send the manuscript out to the publisher.

I want to thank Karen Milner, executive editor at John Wiley & Sons, who greeted my book proposal with those most coveted words: "This is a book we've been waiting for!" Karen has been a true partner—supportive, enthusiastic, and most insightful in her editorial suggestions. The production editor, Pauline Ricablanca, was also most accommodating. The entire Wiley team lived up to the firm's reputation as one of the best publishing organizations. I look forward to the prospect of doing more books with John Wiley.

My sons—Bart and Ben—have been strong supporters of this book and of my career. I am remarkably proud of both of them. Bart is now senior vice president of our company, overseeing our Vancouver office. Ben, who is in advertising, helped design the cover of this book, with some final touches by Wiley.

Marc Egnal, my husband, has been my soul mate in the creation of this work. As a historian who has written four major books, he willingly read draft after draft of this text—with such a finely chiseled editorial touch that I would typically ask him after reading each chapter, "Is there anything left of it?" Happily what remains is distilled and much improved.

Harvard Business School Publishing gave permission to use two chapters that were previously published in the *Harvard Management Communication Letter*. They are "Taking the Jar Out of Jargon," in the August 2001 issue, and "You are the Best Visual," in the October 2001 issue.

To all my readers: Enjoy! And please share with me your thoughts and successes. You can reach me at www.thehumphreygroup.com.

INTRODUCTION

SPEAKING AS AN ACT
OF LEADERSHIP

This book has been written for one reason: to show readers how to lead every time they speak.

In our work with executives, managers, specialists, and professionals over the past 23 years, The Humphrey Group has seen that the most effective leaders use every speaking opportunity to influence and inspire. They make every formal speech, presentation, phone call, or elevator conversation a leadership opportunity. They realize that their power lies less in any title they hold than in their ability to move others. They realize that the true task of a leader is to create believers.

This day-in, day-out commitment to energizing others can be challenging. It means that every conversation, regardless of the task at hand, regardless of the challenges to be surmounted, regardless of the venue or audience, must be thought of as an occasion not merely to inform, but to inspire. It means that a leader must always be ready to convey the right message to a variety of audiences—employees, senior management, customers, partners, and other stakeholders. For a leader, the mike is always on.

This book puts communication squarely at the center of leadership, and shows you how to lead when you speak. It provides a template for speaking as a leader every time you interact with others.

The Challenges

The link between leading and communicating is unmistakable. When people fail to communicate, they fail to lead. It's that simple. You can have brilliant ideas, but if you can't get them across in a way that engages, excites, and motivates others to believe and act, those ideas will remain unrealized. And as a leader you will have missed an opportunity to create followers.

In my years of coaching managers and executives, I've seen many people come to us because they cannot reach others. Here are some examples.

- A senior manager says she's not "heard" when she makes a presentation. Executives interrupt her, and only when others repeat her remarks are they affirmed.
- An engineer with great technical skills has fallen off the fast track because he communicates so poorly.
- An executive faces a rebellion in the ranks because his employees resent his harsh style and insulting messages.
- A brilliant technology specialist who has discovered a new way of building fiber networks is unable to present his ideas to senior executives.

- A CFO cannot ask her managers to speak at senior-level meetings because they don't know how to get their point across clearly and simply.

- An account manager appears dismissive and arrogant when talking to his client. The client has given him 30 days to "shape up" or be removed from the account.

All these individuals are *potential* leaders. Whether they are technology specialists, account managers, or financial executives, they must be able to persuade others to believe in their ideas and act upon them. Failure to engage and influence others means a failure to lead.

My experience as a communication coach has taught me that such examples are not the exceptions; they are the norm. The vast majority of people do not speak as leaders. They may have valuable insights and proposals, but if they can't bring them forward and move others to believe in these ideas, they are not speaking as leaders.

The New Organization

More than ever, organizations are driven by ideas, not by hierarchies. In fact, companies today must be idea driven to succeed in the increasingly competitive business environment. You cannot expect consumers to purchase your products or praise your services simply because they did so last year. The competitive advantage of organizations lies in the know-how of their brightest people. Jack Welch, the former CEO of General Electric (GE), put it this way: "Business is all about getting the best ideas from everyone. New ideas are the lifeblood of the organization."[1] One big idea can shape success for a division, or for a whole company. Just think of an advertising executive, or a software engineer, or a brilliant researcher. Not only must these creative minds think clearly, and articulate that thinking so others buy into it, but managers and business heads must translate these path-breaking ideas into business plans, and sell these to their superiors, to their customers, and to their employees. Everyone, at every level, must bring forward ideas. Noel Tichy, in his book *The Leadership Engine*, states: "Winning leaders understand that ideas are an essential tool for shaping and motivating an organization. They consider the generation of ideas one of their most important functions."[2]

Hierarchies are flattening, so leadership opportunities are plentiful in everyday interactions at every level. Senior leaders have a broad range of possibilities for communicating their ideas. These go well beyond the usual staged events, and require a mind-set that constantly searches for opportunities to sell one's message. The head of a major retail chain, Marc Chouinard, understood the power of seizing such everyday opportunities. He took time to meet with store employees in 20 locations when the company was going through a major restructuring. He knew that his power base resided with those individuals. He spoke clearly, from the heart, and without the claptrap of visual aids. He then turned the discussion over to his audience, and engaged in an open dialogue with them. He won them over, and they implemented the restructuring plan successfully. As he put it, "Thanks to those conversations, they own the plan!"

You don't have to be a C-level officer to speak as a leader in every interaction. A vice president told me of a young woman from his bank's branch who was asked to sit in on a meeting with very senior financial people. Millions of dollars needed to be transferred by this corporate accounting group, and this top team, including the bank's chief accountant, didn't know how to do this. Only the young woman from the branch knew how. She spoke clearly about what needed to be done and provided the leadership needed to orchestrate this transfer. The vice president said: "I remember thinking this is amazing. The most junior person is overseeing the move of millions of dollars. It showed me that anybody at any level can be a good leader."

If you internalize the idea that speaking as a leader is an ever-present responsibility you have to your stakeholders, you will infuse all your speaking with the quality of leadership. Whether you are answering a question, commenting on a project, presenting a strategic plan, selling to a customer, or simply taking a group of people through a solution to a problem, your intention must be to inspire and move others to believe and act on that belief.

The ability to take the stage and lead gives you the power to inspire, influence, and move others. It gives your audience the incentive to listen, respond, and follow. If you accept this role, you will flourish as a leader. But remember: your ability to play this part well depends on your powers of persuasion. Those are the skills that you will discover in this book. As a leader, know that you have a right to speak strongly and with confidence. And know that others want to be convinced, want to be moved, and want to be inspired. While respecting your superiors, get used to this new leadership order in which you are the equal of anyone in your organization.

The Leadership Model™

But how do you speak as a leader in all situations? This book presents a systematic approach called The Leadership Model™. It is scalable: it works equally for an address to a town hall event and for a brief elevator conversation. It unlocks your leadership potential every time you communicate. The Leadership Model consists of four steps: (1) think like a leader, (2) create a leader's script, (3) use the language of leadership, and (4) achieve a leader's presence.

These four steps also structure the four parts of this book. Here are the steps.

1. **Think like a leader.** This first step is mental preparation. You must begin with a vision of leadership, one that sees every speaking situation as an opportunity to motivate others. That vision of leadership requires deep conviction, courage, and a willingness to think beyond hierarchies. The best leaders know their audience, are concerned with inspiring rather than simply informing, and above all are committed to communicating every time they speak. They also know the importance of listening well and learning from others.

2. **Create a leader's script.** The script structures your ideas and influences the audience's thinking. It opens with a grabber that captures the audience's attention. Next comes a clear statement of your subject. But the most important element of The Leader's Script is its message. It's the powerful idea that you want your audience to hear, believe in, and act upon. A leader then supports the message with a persuasive structure, and closes the script with a call to action.

3. **Use the language of leadership.** The best leaders are conscious of the language they use, and deliberately choose words that have the power to influence and inspire. You will learn how to bring your messages to life with language that's clear, conversational, personal, eloquent, and strong. If your words embody these qualities, your ideas will be understood and felt by the audience.

4. **Achieve a leader's presence.** A leader, like a good actor, brings a script to life through energy, eye contact, gestures, and voice. The most compelling speakers realize they are their own best visual. Developing a leader's presence is important whether you are speaking to hundreds or to one person.

The four steps of The Leadership Model provide a powerful template. They will help turn your listeners into followers.

Putting The Leadership Model into Practice

Clients sometimes ask, "How can I possibly internalize The Leadership Model sufficiently to make it work when I'm speaking on the fly?" I tell them, the more you use it, the more instinctive it becomes. It will create small, daily acts of speaking as a leader. This Leadership Model fosters a way of thinking and communicating that enables those who use it to be inspirational in every conversation.

As mentioned above, The Leadership Model is scalable. It is applicable to both a brief phone call with a client and a 30-minute keynote address to 500 executives. Different situations, to be sure, call for different scripts. But the process and overall model are always the same.

No book by itself can completely transform an individual, but this one is designed to be a change agent. *Speaking as a Leader* will take you to a new level of leadership—to where you speak not only about what you know, but more importantly about what you believe and want others to believe. We have all heard speakers who leave us with a lasting, positive impression—they are not necessarily charismatic in the traditional sense of the word. They may not have the "flash" that some others have. But they speak sincerely, deeply, and with passion about what they believe. They speak in a way that engages others, and moves them. They are the leaders of the twenty-first century.

Speaking as a Leader will enable you to achieve this power by bringing forward your ideas and expressing them with clarity, confidence, and *true* charisma. You will learn how to communicate every day with well-focused, clearly developed messages. You will learn how to mobilize others through the power of your ideas. You will learn how to lead every time you speak.

STEP 1

THINK LIKE A LEADER

- ◆ Begin with Vision
- ◆ Think beyond Hierarchies
- ◆ Move from Information to Inspiration
- ◆ Move from Negatives to Positives
- ◆ Speak with Conviction
- ◆ Listen, Listen, Listen
- ◆ Commit to Communicating

CHAPTER 1

BEGIN WITH VISION

In *Alice's Adventures in Wonderland*, Alice says to the Cheshire Cat:

> "Would you tell me, please, which way I ought to go from here?"
>
> "That depends a good deal on where you want to get to," said the Cat.
>
> "I don't much care where—" said Alice.
>
> "Then it doesn't matter which way you go," said the Cat.[1]

Alice discovered that having a larger goal—a broad vision—is all-important. Any leader who says "I don't much care" when asked where he or she wants to go is never going to get anywhere. Leaders need a mission that guides them and their followers.

And it should shape everything a leader communicates. To speak like a leader you must have a clear sense of your larger goal. Begin with vision.

Why a Vision Is Important

A vision tells everyone in your organization, your department, or your area what's important. It shapes, or should shape, all your communications, from major speeches to the way you conduct meetings. It aligns your remarks with the overall goals of your organization. Without a vision, even e-mails can become unproductive. Recently The Humphrey Group worked with a tech company where a group of five engineers sent a total of 17 e-mails back and forth about the specifications of a screen display for a smartphone. A supplier had sent them the wrong product. Should they use it or demand a replacement? There was endless debate about the right course of action. What those five engineers had forgotten, or never grasped fully, was the company's broad vision, which states: "We have an unalterable commitment to the highest quality products." Had they kept this vision in mind, decision making (and their e-mails) would have been far more straightforward. They could have decided—after rigorous testing—that the substitute screens met the company standards, or they could have rejected those screens as substandard. The vision would have led them to the right action.

Visions shape everything leaders say and do, whether they are running a meeting or responding to a question. And there are times when it's useful to restate that vision. One individual I coached remarked that he had begun to do so. In his words: "I find it really valuable to say, at some point in the meeting, 'Let me take a minute to share my vision with you.'" Doing so will rally your audience around your high-level leadership thinking.

Visions Begin at the Enterprise Level

Every organization—as well as groups within an organization—should have a clear vision. These visionary statements should begin at the enterprise level. The vision of other groups must be nested inside that larger vision.

Sergey Brin, co-founder of Google, explained his company's overarching goal this way: "We take all the world's information and make it accessible and useful to everyone. That's our mission, and that's a pretty important mission."[2] Mark Zuckerberg, founder of Facebook, has a simple, clear, and powerful statement. He's even written his company's vision on the inside of his hoodie: "Making the world more open and connected."[3]

It's not just the largest firms that have vision statements. The Humphrey Group, too, has a clear goal: "The Humphrey Group fosters inspirational leadership." That mission helps us stand out in the marketplace—and it shapes this book.

So your mandate is to be a visionary.

Develop Your Vision

Before you speak, know the guiding vision for your company, division, or team. This will keep everyone on the same page. If your team or division does not have a vision, it's useful to formulate one. (These same principles apply if you are creating a vision for the entire enterprise.) Think about where you want your company, department, or team to be in five months, five years—maybe even five decades! To ensure your vision is inspiring, develop it with the following principles in mind.

1. Your Vision Must Be Focused

Consider the following vision statement, delivered to a board of directors:

> It is time to rethink our business strategy and make some dramatic changes. We must bring more focus and discipline to our business. We have a strong entrepreneurial culture, which must operate with a better mix of discipline and aggression. We must rededicate ourselves to profitable growth, and to the overall success of this firm.

This may be an impassioned statement, but it contains at least three messages. Which one is most important? Which one is going to take priority? Multiple messages confuse, rather than inspire. If, instead, the statement had focused on one of these ideas, the speaker would have been clearer. A one-sentence vision statement is always best. Keep it focused.

2. Your Vision Must Be Positive

Lift up your listeners. Move them from "negatives" to "positives." One of the great corporate visions is that of Kinross Gold Corporation. It reads: "Our core purpose is to lead the world in generating value through responsible mining."[4] This high-ground vision infuses everything with the dignity of creating value by acting responsibly—including having respect for local cultures, for employees, for the land being mined, and for everything in the work environment.

A similar positive vision should be a source of inspiration for each division or group within an enterprise. In the example above, the vision for the Finance Group might be "To help the company generate value through responsible financial reporting to all stakeholders."

A manager of a mine in the company might have as her vision "to ensure that the mine generates value by acting responsibly toward employees, suppliers, the local community, and the environment."

Together these "nested" visions support one common and positive corporate goal. As a leader you must always be guided by a larger goal.

3. Your Vision Must Be Attainable

"Becoming the number-one North American oil and gas producer" may be possible if you're now number three. But if your total holdings are one non-producing well, you're probably overreaching. If your vision is not achievable, then the people who work for you will become demoralized. This isn't to say that you can't reach for the moon—John F. Kennedy inspired the American people to do just that—but if that's your vision, be prepared to build rocket ships. Credibility is a well that quickly runs dry when you're stretching the truth.

4. Your Vision Should Reflect the Scope of Your Mandate

No important areas of your organization should fall outside your vision. Agrium, a global company that produces fertilizers and related chemical products, provides a good example of a broad-based mandate. Their sustainability vision is: "Agrium will make an increasingly positive impact on shareholders while helping to feed the world responsibly."[5] Imagine if they had left out the word "increasingly."

That would have excluded from this defining statement one crucial goal—the company's commitment to growing shareholder value by providing increasingly positive returns.

Communicate Your Vision

It is of no use to have a clear and compelling vision if you do not communicate it to *all* your stakeholders. Michael Dell, CEO of Dell Inc., writes in his autobiography, *Direct from Dell*, that "over time, we have developed a laser-focused strategy that we take great pains to communicate consistently and thoroughly throughout the entire global organization." In fact, "at Dell, what ties us all together is belief in our direct model."[6] Whether you head a company, a business unit, or a team, communicating your company's vision is your responsibility. It must be burned in your mind and the mind of every employee, customer, and stakeholder.

So place yourself in the tradition of leaders who speak with a vision that is focused, positive, attainable, and encompassing, and let that vision shape *everything* you deliver. Commit to it in your speeches, presentations, meetings, and off-the-cuff comments. A vision is a living thing: if you broadcast it continually, in all your interactions, others will believe in it, act on it, and with your leadership turn your vision into a reality.

CHAPTER 2

THINK BEYOND HIERARCHIES

In Anton Chekhov's short story "Fat and Thin," two childhood friends greet each other warmly at a railway station after decades apart. The thin man boasts of his accomplishments as a civil servant. But as soon as he learns that the fat man is a much higher-ranking official, he becomes pale and nervous, and starts calling the fat man "Your Excellency." The fat man, saddened by his old friend's sudden fawning behavior, turns and leaves.[1]

This is the power of hierarchies: they can turn people into pale shadows of their former selves. I have seen managers come undone when presenting to senior executives. Instead of providing guidance, they stumble through a dull, information-based presentation and as soon as the executives begin asking questions or making comments, the junior presenters allow the executives to take over. Why? Because these individuals defer to those above them and assume that "leaders" and "followers" are determined by rank. But too often the senior executives are not impressed. Indeed, such performances can be career limiting.

Organizations still do have tops and bottoms. But leaders at all levels must be willing to influence others, even those they don't have authority over. The old structures, where a few at the top had access to all pertinent information and issued orders through a command-and-control structure, are gone. Regardless of your place in the hierarchy, you have a responsibility to lead. But leading takes a different shape depending on whether you are speaking to those who report to you, your peers, or someone more senior than you.

Leading from Above

Leading from above is the most common form of leadership and it's the one we are most familiar with. There are still old-style command-and-control bosses out there. But few are successful in the new world of knowledge workers. Those who think that position equals command run the risk of alienating employees. They don't inspire their workers, and they won't benefit from the flow of knowledge that must move freely in every direction within a corporation.

The best bosses provide a vision that helps direct their company, division, or area. They convey that vision by persuasion, not by preemptive commands. And when forming their views and guiding their employees, they listen carefully. They welcome suggestions, encourage frank conversations, and are open to constructive challenges to their views. James Gorman, CEO of Morgan Stanley, according to one industry colleague, has the ability "to form his ideas and then sell them to the people involved, as opposed to trying to use the power of the assignment to make them do what he wanted."[2] It's this ability that all leaders need.

If a boss is curt or abrupt with employees, heads will shake as soon that executive leaves the room. I once observed a new CEO who was the keynote speaker at a daylong company meeting. Five hundred sales employees were in the hall, waiting expectantly for their new leader. The CEO began by saying, "I can't talk with you for very long . . . I have to go meet with our major shareholders." Then, showing little respect for his audience, he delivered a few rambling comments. He left his audience unimpressed and uninspired.

Think of BP's former CEO Tony Hayward, who got into trouble by saying, after the Deepwater Horizon oil disaster, "there's no one who wants this thing over more than I do. I'd like my life back."[3] Public outcry over these remarks was so great that he was forced to make a second statement apologizing for his words: "My first priority is doing all we can to restore the lives of the people of the Gulf region and their families—to restore their lives, not mine."[4]

Hayward's mistake was extreme, but not out of character with some of the attitudes I've seen when coaching executives. One vice president told me: "I am the one that has to make decisions, and people come to me to hear me say either 'yes' or 'no.' Sometimes two people come and fight it out in front of me for my approval . . . I like the smell of blood!" Another executive liked to toy with his subordinates. As a young woman explained: "My boss makes me so upset. When I go in to see him he plays with me—flirts, makes suggestive comments, banters, and tries to throw me off guard. When I attempt to bring the discussion to the subject at hand, he is cold and indifferent. He could not care less about my projects . . . yet I need to get approval for my programs." Such executives are using their power to intimidate and diminish their subordinates. They are not leaders; they are bullies.

Leadership is not about *you* and your power, your life, or your seniority. With authority comes the responsibility to guide, inspire, learn from, and support those you lead. A good example of such leadership came from a client who told me the following story.

> When I was a young analyst at a bank I had the opportunity to be part of a senior level meeting. Sitting next to me was the executive vice president and treasurer of the bank. At first I felt very small and unimportant next to that executive. But when I spoke, that executive turned directly to me, squared his shoulders with mine, and gave me his full attention. I felt so valued by him and by the bank. I will never forget it.

Fortunately, today's organizations offer lots of opportunities to lead from above. E-mail, conference calls, meetings—every day you have an opportunity to motivate your team and let them know that their contributions are valuable. If you are at the top of your organization or simply the manager of a team, communicating with your team members is critical. A recent study by Google revealed that these communication skills are far more important for Google managers than their technical skills. The manager's ability to coach employees and provide constructive feedback in one-on-one meetings ranked number one while technical skills ranked dead last (number seven).[5] Leading from above is more important than it has ever been. It requires a guiding hand and communications that encourage and recognize staff achievement.

Leading from the Side

In today's flatter organizations you'll often find that you have to lead your peers, clients, or suppliers. Instead of working from the top down or bottom up, you must inspire from the *side*. Leading from the side can be challenging. You don't have the authority to tell peers what to do, so you must sell your ideas to them, find common ground, and build a productive relationship.

The first rule in this situation is to abandon the "us and them" mentality. One advertising firm's account manager we coached had trouble dealing with clients who were essentially on the same level that he was. As he saw it, he was usually right and the client was usually wrong. He remarked: "I'll be sitting in the room with five people from the client firm and they are taking a position that is dead wrong. They're telling me how to present their brand. They don't realize that I'm the expert." But as we role-played the situation, he came to understand that he could only lead if he listened well and responded fully to the concerns he heard.

Another good guideline: try to see yourself through the other person's eyes. I coached an engineer who complained of constant arguments with a colleague in sales. I asked him, "So how do you think this colleague sees you?" This took the engineer by surprise—he had never stopped to consider how the world looked from his colleague's point of view. Then he laughed, and said, "Well, my colleague in sales is probably thinking 'Great—here he goes with another technical explanation of how we can't go to market because we haven't fixed all the bugs yet. But by the time we fix all the bugs, our window of opportunity for sales will be gone!'" The engineer continued, "So I guess I haven't really been listening to *him*." Once he started thinking about the project from his colleague's point of view, he was able to bridge their differences and find a way to move forward—together.

Still another principle for leading your peers is to pitch your arguments in terms of common goals. One individual, Jeanette, whom we in The Humphrey Group have worked with, described the breakthrough conversation she had with a fellow manager. She said to her colleague, "Mohinder, I'd like to work with you on getting this project off the ground, and make it a win-win for both our groups and the company. There are huge challenges to this project, and I believe that working together we can tackle them head-on." The two of them cooperating became far more effective than either could be individually. Jeanette's outreach is an example of what we mean by leading from the side.

Leading from Below

Leading from below is one of the most difficult forms of leading, and requires confidence and diplomacy. But it is vital for the health of any organization, and is worth practicing (if you're in a junior position) and fostering (if you're in a senior position). I work with more and more executives who *want* their juniors to lead them. But too many employees feel overwhelmed by an authority figure, so they respond in a variety of inappropriate ways—none of which benefits their boss, their company, or even their own careers.

Some managers become timid and undercut themselves when presenting to their bosses. I worked with a manager of logistics who often brought appeals to more senior people for funds. These conversations, he admitted, were difficult. He went into these meetings with an insecure mind-set, assuming his superiors wouldn't agree with him. He would begin by saying, "I won't take much of your time" or "You may not want to hear this." And it was downhill from there. We worked on creating a more positive, confident tone for these interactions. Rather than sounding like he was pleading for funds, he began to sound like he was leading his executives to make the right decision.

Other people become defensive or aggressive when they attempt to lead from below, an approach that rarely succeeds. Here's an example:

> BOSS: I'm asking you to get more out of your people. We are in a period of cost containment, and I think your group can improve its productivity.
>
> EMPLOYEE: Get more out of my people? How is that possible? They are already working 110 percent. We've lost three people, and now they have to be replaced or I won't be able to meet the demands.

This employee has lost a great opportunity to influence her boss. She might have said:

> EMPLOYEE: I see your point. I've worked out the numbers to save $15 million in our division, but I'm going to need to hire a person in cost accounting to help me implement the program. When you have time, I'd like to go over the numbers with you.

Still other people fail to lead from below because they get trapped by their own intellectual superiority. They think they have the right answers, and they think their executives have less knowledge and therefore are wrong. As one vice president put it to me: "Our senior executives have meetings every Monday to see what the company should do and invariably they come up with some harebrained ideas that must be responded to." With that approach, the vice president's ideas were sure to be rejected.

Finally, some people have difficulty leading from below because their upbringing makes them feel it would be presumptuous to do so. One female client said her father had told her to "keep her head down," or she would be like a nail sticking out from a board—ready to be hammered.

What's the answer? How do you best lead from below?

1. **Be political.** Practice speaking to your superiors with confidence, but with respect. These are skills everyone needs to master. Even CEOs report to the board.

2. **Be direct.** Executives don't want you to beat around the bush. An individual in one of our seminars was faced with the prospect of having to tell his CEO that, because of human error, one of the company's largest producing oil wells had to be shut down. Some managers would have tried to avoid such a discussion, or soft-pedaled the reality. But this individual went boldly into the CEO's office, told him what had happened, explained how the mistake had cost the company $6 million, and most importantly outlined what needed to be done. The CEO hit the roof and made his feelings known in unmistakable language. But in the end the manager got what he wanted: the CEO's permission to spend several million dollars to drill another hole. This is leadership. Did the head of the company want to spend that extra money? No. But he did because the manager persuaded him it was the wisest step to take.

3. **Be bold.** It may mean speaking up more frequently at a meeting of senior colleagues, initiating a one-on-one discussion, or seizing the opportunities to lead from below when the opportunity strikes.

I first learned the power of boldness when I was a speechwriter at Nortel Networks (then called Northern Telecom). I was asked to write for the top officers. Since this was my first corporate job, I could have been very deferential. But my boss, Roy Cottier, said: "You go in and talk to those executives about what they should say . . . how they should present their ideas . . . then sell them on your vision for that speech." He did add a note of political caution: "Be respectful of their position, and their views, and show them how the speech will reflect their own thinking and goals." Cottier taught me to think of myself as an adviser rather than simply a writer. That political intelligence has served me well in my career working with top executives. Being a speechwriter was a great way to learn how to lead from below.

Every conversation within an organization—or outside it—is an opportunity to shape your audience's thinking, no matter what your job title or theirs. It often requires different skills to lead from above, from the side, or from below, but leaders need to be effective in all these relationships. Succeeding on these different stages isn't always easy—it requires emotional sensitivity, political intelligence, tact, and courage. But if you see every conversation as a leadership opportunity, you will soon develop the skills that you need to become a successful leader.

CHAPTER 3

MOVE FROM INFORMATION TO INSPIRATION

Why do some people bore their audiences, while others turn their listeners into believers? One key difference is that poor speakers are stuck in an *informational* mode, while more compelling speakers command an *inspirational* style. The informational mode emphasizes content, while the inspirational mode reflects a commitment to an idea or vision.

In his book *Lincoln at Gettysburg*, Garry Wills discusses these two modes of speaking. Wills contrasts the remarks of Edward Everett, a long-winded politician, with those of Abraham Lincoln. Everett was the first to speak at the dedication ceremony of the National Cemetery in Gettysburg, and gave an informational address. His talk lasted three hours and covered in painstaking detail the entire three-day battle. In contrast, Lincoln followed with his brief "Gettysburg Address," now recognized as one of the finest speeches in the English language. This talk lasted less than three minutes, and unlike Everett's remarks, it offered few details. As Wills puts it, Lincoln's "speech hovers far above the carnage . . . The discussion is driven back and back, beyond the historical particulars, to great ideals that are made to grapple naked in an airy battle of the mind."[1]

While neither pure information nor pure inspiration is ideal, most speakers err on the side of presenting too many facts, as Everett did. If you want to be a leader, you should, like Lincoln, have a message or vision that drives your talk. You should move from information to inspiration.

Why So Many Speakers Use the Informational Approach

Speakers are stuck in the "content" mode for a variety of reasons. In each case a misconception leads to this data-heavy approach.

Misconception #1: Presenting Information without a Strong Argument is Safe

Some people feel that it's safer to say nothing—simply present the facts. They worry about the dangers of making bold statements. They feel they can avoid criticism if they just provide "useful" data about their topic. Or they feel it would be presumptuous to present an argument to their boss or their board. These presenters move through mounds of information, with no apparent purpose or point of view, until they get to the last slide of their presentation and the eureka moment when they say, "So what I am saying is . . ." Unfortunately the audience is asleep by then.

Misconception #2: Presenting a Data-loaded Talk Shows that a Person is an Expert

Many professionals and managers, especially those with a technology, legal, or financial background, want to show their expertise. They focus their remarks on what they *know*, rather than what they *believe*. They can tell you the virtues of GSM, and why it's superior to TDMA and CDMA.[2] Much of their presentation is weighed down with acronyms and jargon. Of course, there are times when technical details are needed. But too often they're not. And those presenters, rather than impressing their listeners, simply lose them.

What these presenters don't realize is that data by itself is rarely useful, and that their listeners want coherence, not piles of information. That's true at every level, from specialists and managers to the members of the C-suite. All the executives I work with *hate* to receive those information dumps. A chief financial officer once said to me, "I've got too much information. I take it home in my briefcase, it's in my in-basket, in long reports, memos, and e-mails. And I get it in formal presentations, when my people come in, sit down, pull out their visuals, and dump more info on me than I can take home. Now when people come in and start pouring out data, I'll say to them, 'Forget the paper, just talk to me.'"

Misconception #3: The Corporate Culture Demands Information-heavy Presentations

Some people provide data-heavy reports because they see others in the company taking this approach. They attend meetings where they see that every speaker has overloaded slides and no discernible message. They conclude that's what is demanded of them. One client came to us because his boss felt he filled his presentations with too many needless facts. He turned off senior management and failed to get his ideas approved. When I asked him why he felt obliged to present so much detail, he said, "Presentation binders in my last company were four inches thick! The culture dictated that I had to have at least twenty slides." However, such information dumps do not impress. Ultimately, a culture of overloaded presentations is one where messages are lost and productivity suffers.

Misconception #4: I'll Look Unprepared if I Don't Have Lots of Slides

I've heard so many leaders say: "If I don't have a full deck of slides I'll look unprepared." They envision that their audience or their boss will see they only have five slides rather than 15 or 50 and assume that they didn't put enough time or effort into preparing the talk. This need to look and sound prepared becomes almost obsessive the higher up one's audience is. Yet executives are looking for clear thinking—not mounds of slides.

The Informational Approach Turns Up Everywhere

Often the informational approach dominates every form of communication—not only when you are speaking in person, but when you are speaking on paper.

- PowerPoint presentations frequently become information dumps, with no structure and no clear message. In many cases, members of the audience will miss several minutes of your talk because they're trying to decode the information on the screen. Or they simply give up and stop paying attention!

- E-mails and reports are commonly the receptacle of too much information. I have seen an e-mail conversation between a company and one of its vendors that exemplifies this. I would include it here, except that when printed out it is 45 pages long! It is all information, no message—which is precisely why the respondents went back and forth for three months with no resolution. It was forwarded to me by a manager to illustrate what he had to deal with at work. At the top he wrote: "Aargh. This is why I skim but do not read longer e-mails."

- Even voice mail messages can be overburdened with data. Often people begin leaving a message, and are cut off before completing it. Leaders need to get to the point in the allotted time.

So the information dump, which is altogether too common, makes little sense if you want to get your message across in today's fast-paced world.

The Inspirational Approach

The inspirational approach is far superior. When a speaker is in the inspirational mode, he or she moves the audience with the power of an idea, and with the passion that's behind that idea. The inspirational mode is the domain of a leader. A leader should always have a vision or message that transcends the facts. Here's what this mind-set means in everyday situations.

1. Look at every speaking situation as an opportunity to lead, to inspire your audience by presenting an idea or viewpoint they can

accept and act upon. Seen as such, all situations are potentially motivational moments. Use them or lose them.

2. Realize that your true power lies not in content, but in your vision. Francis Bacon may have said "Knowledge is power,"[3] but today the world is drowning in knowledge. What people need is clarity, insight, and interpretive ideas that allow us to make sense of information. If the informational approach is about showing what you know, the inspirational approach is about showing what you believe and want others to believe.

3. Make sure you have an inspiring idea that comes through. Even the best ideas can get lost in a sea of content. Keep your details to a minimum. The principles set down in every chapter in this book, from those on vision, to those on message and structure, to those on presence, will help you focus on that goal.

4. Ask yourself after each event, "Was my audience inspired?" One of my first clients, who became a CEO of a large oil company, told me: "Every time I use your approach, people come up to me and say, 'That was inspiring.'" It's important to gauge whether your goal has been met.

The Power of the Inspirational Approach

Time and again we in The Humphrey Group have seen the remarkable success that comes when speakers move from information to inspiration.

We worked with an engineer, Serge, who had an important presentation to give to top executives in a global company. But he had crafted it with mind-numbing detail. His boss, knowing the executives in the audience would be turned off by such an information dump, asked for our help. The first step was to reinvent the presentation, which called for investing in a new radically designed engine. The text was given a vision, and at least three-quarters of the technical detail was eliminated. We worked on delivery, too.

The day after his presentation, Serge called me, virtually exploding with excitement. His boss, who had been in the audience, was proud. His boss's boss loved it, and, remarkably, the executive vice president in charge of the division came up to him and congratulated him on being "the person for the job."

But the even bigger win was getting approval for $500,000 to continue with this project, and gaining credibility for the division. The fact that Serge's career was now spiraling upward was a final benefit. All this because he had moved from a technical informational approach to discussing an inspirational idea: how the engine would support a corporate-wide commitment to leadership in the industry.

Many other speakers we work with have similar stories. And it's not just in formal situations that you want to move from information to inspiration. It's in everyday leadership "moments." One executive I have worked with is Tom Marinelli, Executive Vice President, Chief Transformation Officer and Chief Technology Officer of the Ontario Lottery and Gaming Corporation (OLG). He told me that "I encourage my people to see that as they move up the organization, they must always be leading—always be on, ready to influence and inspire. As a leader you have to have that mind-set. And when I step into an elevator, I'll be asked a question about the transformation that's underway at OLG, and I feel I must say something clear and inspirational—if I do not, it will be a lost leadership moment. It's challenging, but it becomes easier every time you do it."

Such people have made the move from information to inspiration. People at all levels and in all walks of life can inspire. The word "inspire" may sound like a reach, but it simply means you speak in such a way that you will move people with your thinking. Without inspiration, who would invest in your idea? Who would give you a warm and enthusiastic applause? Who would recommend you for a promotion? The delivery of information will get you none of these results. But if you move from information to inspiration, you are positioning yourself as a leader who can create believers when you speak.

CHAPTER 4

MOVE FROM NEGATIVES TO POSITIVES

For myself I am an optimist—it does not seem to be much use being anything else.[1]
—Winston Churchill

Replace negative thoughts with positive thoughts to create positive results.[2]
—Willie Nelson

If you want to think like a leader, be positive. This outlook should shape your vision and your formal and informal speaking.

The Negativity Trap

One of the key characteristics of the most successful leaders—and communicators—is their resolve to always remain positive. Their speeches, presentations, and one-on-one conversations are upbeat. They don't hide from problems: they see them as bumps along the road, not as insurmountable obstacles. And that outlook shapes their communication. They know that leadership involves inspiring others—taking an audience to higher ground, to a place of possibilities.

Negativity undercuts leadership. I know executives who approach major clients saying, "Tell me what we're doing wrong." Instead, they should ask, "What can we do to help you?" or "How can we make our relationship even better?" Negativity, too, often mars one-on-one interactions. A manager might tell a boss, "The accounting department just won't listen to me." Or, "I'm having a terrible time with that supplier." Such statements reflect poorly on the speaker.

Our voice mail greetings also too often are shaped by negatives. ("I'm sorry I'm not here to take your call.") Why apologize? Hopefully, you're doing something more productive than waiting for the next call.

Why are people unnecessarily negative?

1. **They are not political.** Responding to a statement with "I don't agree" or "that's wrong" will only create poor relations.

2. **They let their guard down.** An executive might say at a cocktail event, "I don't know why we hired Joe." But the next day he will regret it.

3. **They lack confidence.** An employee may blurt out "it was nothing" when complimented by a boss for doing something well.

4. **They share their fears.** A candidate for a job may say: "Quite honestly, I'm not sure I can make the transition from the public to the private sector. But I'd like to try." What interviewer will hire someone who is not sure of the fit?

5. **They know about a negative situation, and come forward to describe it even when they're not asked to do so.** Saying "we expect to make some changes in our management team" will put everyone on edge, wondering if their boss is being fired.

6. **They just can't resist the temptation to focus on problems.** A client told me: "Whenever my boss speaks to me, he has something negative to say. He promoted me, but said it was despite the fact that one of my accounts was losing money."

Resist the temptation to be negative. Negatives bring people down, rather than lifting them up. If you want to lead when you speak, stay on the high ground.

From Negative to Positive

Adhere to the rules below, and you'll be positive—and positively inspiring!

Rule # 1: Avoid Unnecessary Negatives

Learn to avoid the negative traps listed above. All the situations described involve bringing forward a negative when you're not required to do so.

Rule #2: In a Negative Situation, Look to the Positive

There are certain situations where negatives are a reality. Leaders acknowledge them, but find a way to move toward the positive. For example, let's say the chief financial officer of a company has to break the news that the remainder of the year will be a difficult one for the company. That statement should be followed by steps the company is taking to meet the challenge.

One of the most stirring examples of the ability to remain positive, even in the face of adversity, is the speech delivered by baseball great, Lou Gehrig. He spoke on July 4, 1939, just after he learned that he had ALS, now often called "Lou Gehrig's disease." In this farewell address he began by saying, "Fans, for the past two weeks you have been reading about a bad break I got. Yet today I consider myself the luckiest man on the face of the earth." He went on to enumerate the many ways he felt lucky. And ended: "I have an awful lot to live for!"[3] Even when confronting grave challenges, leaders stay positive.

BP chairman Carl-Henric Svanberg, in his letter to shareholders in the company's 2010 annual report, looked to the positive. After acknowledging the realities of the Deepwater Horizon oil spill, Svanberg concluded: "While we face substantial challenges, shareholders must be in no doubt—BP has the determination and strength needed to restore its reputation and deliver long-term shareholder value."[4] This is a great leadership statement.

Rule #3: Focus on Solutions, Not Problems

Leaders solve problems. If you are speaking about a challenging situation, acknowledge the problem, but emphasize the solution. No one would be inspired by an executive whose message is, "We've had a terrible year," or "I've never seen morale so low." It's much better to say, "We've put plans in place for turning this company around—and I can tell you they're working," or "We've listened, and I know all of you will be pleased by the programs we've initiated to foster employee development." The point here is not simply to have a "sunny disposition," but to take a solutions-oriented approach. Don't communicate until you've come up with an action plan, or at least until you can point your listeners in the right direction.

This guideline should also shape your key messages. For example, don't say, "While I have every reason to believe in our company's future, it was a difficult year for us." It's better to state, "While it was a difficult year for our company, I have every reason to believe in our future." Build to the positive in your scripts. Leave your audience on the high ground.

Rule #4: Spend More Time on the Positive

Being positive doesn't mean adopting the foolish optimism of Dr. Pangloss, one of the heroes of Voltaire's novel *Candide*. Dr. Pangloss kept repeating, "All is for the best," as terrible things happened around him. [5] You should acknowledge the negatives, but don't dwell on them. Perform this simple check: examine your speech, presentation, or remarks to see whether you spend more time on what's favorable or unfavorable. Make certain the balance tips heavily to the positive side.

Rule # 5: Keep Your Language Positive

Realize that the words you use set the tone for people's thinking. So use positive language. Instead of saying "We have a problem," say "We have a challenge" or "We have an opportunity." Replace complaints with action statements and double negatives with positives. Instead of saying "It's not impossible," say "We can do it!" Replace "no problem" with "I'm pleased to help you." Change your phone message from "I'm sorry I can't come to the phone" to "Please leave a message."

Every time you speak, you're shaping a reality in your audience's mind. Negatives lead listeners into a realm of doubt, uncertainty, and failure. Lift up your audience and you will inspire them.

CHAPTER 5

SPEAK WITH CONVICTION

The most effective leaders communicate with conviction. Your vision provides direction, but your conviction shows the strength of your viewpoint. When you speak with conviction, the way you present your material says, "This is something I believe. This message is important to me . . . and should be to you."

Conviction does not come from tricks. I once met a speech coach who suggested that his students wink at their audience every once in a while. Another directed her female protégés to wear bright red lipstick. Some public speaking coaches engage in less theatrical but similarly superficial advice, such as telling presenters to keep their hands above their waist. Such gimmicks bear no relationship to leadership and they encourage would-be leaders to rely on theatrics to create an impression.

The job of a leader is to inspire people and to energize them into action. Where is that life, that energy, going to come from if not from you? Conviction comes from within you. Leaders who show their conviction have passion, authenticity, courage, and honesty.

Be Passionate

To begin with, conviction involves speaking with passion. Audiences know when a speaker lacks passion. The delivery is lifeless and monotone. No wonder listeners tune out, play with their smartphones, or simply doze. To speak with passion, you must think about every word you're delivering, and convey its importance.

We teach leaders how to deliver speeches and presentations with passion. We mark up their scripts to emphasize key words and phrases and build in pauses. Even if you only have notes, you should know exactly which words and sentences carry your meaning, and deliver those lines with emphasis. This process for bringing passion to your speaking is described in chapter 22. It will ensure that even when you are reading, you can bring your speech to life.

Harry Truman spoke with passion to the American Society of Newspaper Editors, and the result was electrifying. Guided only by his mental notes, he talked (according to one account) "in his own vocabulary, out of his own humor and his own heart." Truman spoke "in earnestness . . . with each man in the hall. He was suddenly a very interesting man of great candor who discussed the problems of American leadership with men as neighbors." It was this speech that gave rise to the epithet "Give 'em Hell, Harry."[1] He said exactly what he thought and believed, and it was this commitment to speaking with passion that helped him win the 1948 presidential campaign.

Speaking with passion is important every time you open your mouth at a meeting. Show your passion for your ideas by expressing them with a committed tone, strong words, and compelling arguments. Keep this in mind: *your audience will only feel passion for your ideas if you show that passion.* The best ideas, presented in a ho-hum manner, will fall on deaf ears.

Speaking with passion, of course, begins with conviction about what you are saying. You cannot fake passion. It involves a conscious effort to show that you are committed to what you are saying. If you speak with passion, your language, ideas, and arguments will make believers out of your listeners. The more you do this, the more people will pay attention when you speak—because they know you're telling them something that's important to you.

Be Authentic

Speaking with conviction also means being authentic. When you convey your authenticity to your listeners, you're telling them, "These ideas are a good fit for me. They emerge from my experience and my deep beliefs." Your audience wants to know that there's a person leading them, not a talking head brought in to repeat a few pat phrases.

Authenticity boosts a leader's credibility and, ultimately, an organization's bottom line. Apple watchers were well aware of Steve Jobs's keen involvement in every product—which time and again made him the perfect person for each new product launch. The same was true of Al Gore's presentations on the environment, or Bono's appeals for aid for developing countries. They are all authentic leaders.

One good indication of your authenticity is your willingness to use the pronoun "I"—and mean it. Tell your audience, "I believe," or "I'm convinced," or "It's my view that . . ." This will lead you into your own authentic self, and it will make a huge difference in the way your words are perceived.

Another way to be authentic is to relate your message to your own life's story. It's often useful to tell stories about yourself. One of our clients, the head of research for a large pharmaceutical company, had to prepare an important speech about genetics and public policy. It could have been a very dry talk. But he put himself into it. He began with the following story.

> When I was 18 years old, I left Canada for England to do my undergraduate and medical studies at Cambridge University. The first week I found myself sitting next to a Nobel Prize–winning biochemist, Lord Todd. I still remember one thing he told me as clearly as though it were yesterday. And that was how he envied the younger generation because he believed that his generation was probably the last to be mortal. Because of the tremendous explosion in science and biology, he expected that future generations would live forever. Tonight I will describe how genetics is dramatically changing the paradigm for medical research.

With that story, the speaker became much more real to his audience.

Jack Welch was a master storyteller and used personal stories to convey a corporate message. Because of his commitment to storytelling, General Electric now has a culture of storytelling.

These narratives, presented by executives and other employees, help convey the vision that guides the company.[2] When you tell a story, you share something personal, and become more real to your audience. You open yourself up to the audience, and they become more open to you.

There is no better example of personal stories than those in Steve Jobs's 2005 commencement address at Stanford University. He begins, "Today I want to tell you three stories from my life. That's it. No big deal. Just three stories."[3] Despite his disclaimer, they are amazing stories, including one that takes us back to his birth: he was the child of an unwed mother who gave him up. And, initially, his adoptive parents didn't want him either because he was the wrong sex. Fortunately, this Dickensian story ends with the enormous success and admirable career Steve Jobs had. Stories like this inspire audiences because they show the vulnerability of a successful business leader.

Your stories don't have to be elaborate. They can be short and snappy. Ted Turner, the media mogul, is known for his witty personal anecdotes. He once told an audience: "my father wanted me to be a big success, and I've been a big success. If I hadn't been a big success, he would kick my ass around for the rest of eternity. I'd never get any rest. Even if I was in heaven, it'd be hell."[4] Sharing something personal with your audience adds authenticity to your message, and encourages listeners to be more receptive to what you are saying.

Be Courageous

Leaders who speak with conviction are also courageous. They recognize that, at times, they must bring forward messages that may encounter opposition. That's a challenge that can be difficult for even the strongest leaders. Leaders increasingly require courage to deliver difficult messages as their organizations experience unprecedented change. Sometimes they must tell people they could lose their jobs, at other times they need to present a new vision to a staff that has become comfortable with the old.

Strong leaders look for courage in those they hire. Michael Dell writes in his autobiography that when he interviews candidates, he almost always "makes a point of actively disagreeing with them. I want to know if they have strong opinions and are willing to defend them. At Dell we need people who are confident enough of their own abilities and strong in their convictions."[5]

Some leaders either avoid difficult conversations or beat around the bush when they have tough messages to deliver. The Humphrey Group has a seminar called *Leadership Conversations*™, and we show managers how to talk to their employees about issues such as poor work habits, inappropriate dress or language, and even bad breath. Such discussions require courage and commitment.

Many leaders who have taken our courses have shown impressive courage. One participant from Jordan told about a time when she was in the room with the king of Jordan and many of his deputies. All of these officials were males. She had done extensive research on the topic under discussion, and she knew that she had an important contribution to make. But she felt like an outsider, and initially failed to voice her views. Then she reflected on what she had done, and the next time she met with the king, she told him about her findings. He was positive and asked for her recommendations. She brought them forward, and they were implemented.

A similar example came from another participant in our *Taking the Stage* seminar for women. She had recently attended a diversity program, and while sitting in an information session sponsored by her firm's management, she realized that every member of the senior management team was a white male. During the Q&A period she summoned up the courage to stand up and ask why this was so. She was trembling when she spoke, but after the session, her voice mail was full. She had messages from male colleagues who said, "Wow. That took courage," and from female colleagues who said, "Go girl!" A few weeks later when the CEO called her in, she went to his office expecting to be fired. Instead, he offered her a promotion, because he saw her as a courageous leader. From there her career took off.

Be Honest

Speaking with conviction also requires honesty. Whether you are speaking to shareholders, to the public, or to your employees, you have an obligation to be clear and honest. Being honest means you must never deceive, misrepresent, or lie. But you don't necessarily have to share everything you know. In fact, there is a sweet spot to honesty—being truthful but not necessarily spilling every detail. Consider this Q&A in which the speaker over-answers:

REPORTER: What will your drilling costs look like over the next few years?

OIL EXECUTIVE: They'll continue upward. There are a lot of cost pressures. Steel prices are up. And drilling rig rates, seismic crew rates will increase. We're facing huge costs and I'm not happy about that. But it's a reality we live with.

This is honesty to a fault, and it paints a negative picture of the company and the leader. Instead, the oil executive should have simply said: "We expect our costs to increase, but will continue to hold them at 30 percent below industry average." That's much more uplifting.

When someone says "to be honest," or "let me be honest with you," or "can I be frank?" what often follows is too negative. Some people think they are being brutally honest, when they're simply being brutal. In reality, honesty from a leader should continue to inspire others. And, as a rule of thumb, avoid expressions like "to be honest," since they imply that everything else you have said is not true.

Effective leaders communicate with conviction. They persuade others because they tap into what's real to them—their passion, authenticity, courage, and honesty. Leaders are held in high esteem because they are seen as having this depth, this strength of character. Speak with conviction, and you are well on your way to becoming a strong, credible leader.

CHAPTER 6

LISTEN, LISTEN, LISTEN

The word *absurdity* comes from the Latin word *surdus*, meaning *deaf* or *mute*. Life makes little sense to those who don't listen. And that's particularly true for leaders, whose role is to guide others. If you want to communicate as a leader, you must be a superb listener.

Listening gives a leader access to powerful ideas—to the information, suggestions, findings, and musings that are the raw material of clarity and change. Today information is widely shared by people at all levels and across the organization. Effective leaders need to gather information from many sources and use it to make the best decisions.

Whether leaders are speaking to a thousand people or to one individual, listening is critical because it gives them a lifeline to their audience. You must understand precisely what concerns and motivates your listeners, or they will never follow you. If there's a mood in the room, you must know it. If you are an executive and your employees have an issue with management, you must understand it. If you are making a sales presentation, your customers must feel your pitch has been designed for them. In short, you must get inside the minds of your audience and shape what you say so that it reaches them. This listening often begins with audience analysis even before you prepare your talk, and it should continue as you engage in dialogue with those in the room.

Listening is a prerequisite to motivational leadership, and successful listening connects you with your audience on three levels—the physical, mental, and emotional.

The Challenges of Listening

If you analyze your habits, you will probably find many ways you could be a better listener. For example, you should improve your listening skills if . . .

- you're a manager who stays in your office, has lunch brought in, and avoids informal contact with your staff.
- you're a sales person who begins a meeting with a prospective client by elaborating on your product or company before asking about the client's need.
- you're an engineer or technical specialist and you focus more on your charts and graphs than on your audience.
- you check your smartphone while an employee is giving a presentation or briefing you on a project.
- you're a senior manager who delivers a presentation on the company's strategy without showing how this strategy will affect those in the room.

- you jump into conversations without hearing what's been said.
- your mind rushes ahead while others are talking to you.

All these situations represent listening lethargy—a failure to grasp what the audience is thinking. To lead you must have followers. And followers are not created by self-absorption or by talking *at* people. Followers are developed by leaders who carefully listen to their audiences and respond fully to their concerns.

For those who acknowledge that listening is critical to leadership, the next question becomes, "How can I listen more effectively?"

Listening on Three Levels

Good listening involves keeping your audience in mind all the time. The best actors accomplish this by listening to their audience while performing. Christopher Newton, former artistic director of the Shaw Festival in Niagara-on-the-Lake, Ontario, Canada, once told an audience of after-dinner guests: "The actor divides his head—one side inside the part, the other focused on the audience."[1] You can be a committed listener if you engage in such active listening on three levels: physical, mental, and emotional. Only by working with these three approaches will you fully come to understand the views of your audience and, more broadly, individuals in your organization.

1. Listen Physically

This first level of listening requires that you create physical openness. Many people shut themselves off physically without realizing it.

To begin with, make sure the space between you and your audience is an open physical environment. Get out of the office and mingle. Go to the employee cafeteria, use the health club, invite your staff to your home for a barbecue. Create circumstances in which you encounter others in more informal settings. And if you do meet with people in your office, don't hide behind a big desk.

In boardrooms and meeting rooms, be mindful that the seat you take reflects your listening skills. If you are at a long boardroom table, and you choose to sit at one end, you signal that you feel you are in control, and may be more interested in talking than listening. More of today's leaders choose to sit at the side of the table to show they do not want to dominate, but want to listen. That's an excellent message to send.

But beware of sitting at the side of a long table if your audience is sitting directly opposite you. This positioning creates a polarity between the two parties, and, in this case, opposites don't attract. If you're part of a group talking to another group, avoid sitting opposite the group you are communicating with. For example, a sales team selling to a prospective client should not all sit opposite the client's team. Instead, they should intermingle with the client's team.

Physical listening begins with where you sit or stand. But that's not all. It is also conveyed through open body language—your posture, eye contact, and expression. The best communicators always pay attention to what their body is saying.

Show you're listening by aligning your body with that of the person you are talking to. Don't speak at an angle to the other person. Your shoulders should be directly parallel to theirs.

Good posture is another way you show you are listening. Individuals who slouch or lean too far back signal they may be self-protective, defensive, or detached. They're not ready to communicate. On the other hand, beware of posture that's too straight. Rigidity of posture may indicate firmness in one's thinking and an inability to open up to the other person's ideas. Good posture involves standing or sitting tall but in a relaxed way. It may even include leaning slightly in the direction of the audience—suggesting that you are listening intently. To show that you're listening, also keep your arms open. If they're folded or your hands are closed, you will not appear receptive. Don't turn your arms into armor. Often people close or fold their arms simply because it's easier for them to think when they do so, or they may feel more relaxed. But the subliminal message sent to the other person is that you are not open—that you are not listening.

Look the other person in the eye, too. The more eye contact you make (without staring) the more likely you are to hear what is being said. And the more the other person will feel that you are listening. Remember that if you avert your eyes to shuffle papers or look at your watch or smartphone, you will convey the same message: that you are not engaged.

A warm, interested expression on your face will also indicate that you are listening. Nodding your head (as opposed to nodding off) further suggests your involvement. And responding with facial expressiveness will show that you are listening and that you've internalized what the speaker has said. Body language says a lot about the kind of relationship you have with others.

2. Listen Mentally

The second level of listening involves mental engagement. As Ernest Hemingway wrote: "When people talk, listen completely. Most people never listen."[2] So listen closely to the ideas and concerns of your audience.

Mental listening should begin even before you enter the room. Any presentation you make or conversation you have should be guided by a keen sense of audience. And you can only have that sense of audience if you listen in advance. Ask yourself before you write a speech, prepare a presentation, or walk into a meeting, "What is my audience thinking about the topic I will address?" Then ask yourself, "How can I move my audience from point A to point B mentally?" Few leaders ask these questions, and for this reason they often fail to reach their audience.

Once you are in the room, there's a need for more mental listening. At its most fundamental level, mental listening requires deep concentration on what the other person or group is saying. Too many times people rush ahead in their mind to form a conclusion, rather than hearing the other person out. The danger of this is that they may form false conclusions and misinterpret what's being said.

The best leaders listen with an open mind in all their encounters— no matter where in the corporate hierarchy that information might be coming from. Jamie Dimon, CEO of JPMorgan Chase & Co., is a great listener, according to Aaron Scott, an employee. "What set Jamie apart from the rest was that he appreciates ideas. Even though I was seven or more levels from the top, I would, on occasion, send him some idea I had that was bigger than my small department. Without fail, he would respond by thanking me or letting me know that he had passed it on to the appropriate leadership."[3]

Mental listening also involves hearing *everything*. People often edit out the things they don't want to hear. Be open and create a climate in which others are encouraged to tell you the truth.

Mental listening involves building bridges. Draw upon the other person's words. Say: "As I listened to you, I realized that . . ." Or "As I understand your view . . ." Or "I am on side with you regarding . . ." Or simply, "Good point." Tap into the ideas of the other person by probing and enquiring. Test your ideas and preconceptions against the new information being presented. Ask how the other person has reached her conclusions. Interlace observations she has made with your own. In this way, you'll be creating a tapestry of collaborative thinking.

In sum, mental listening, the second tier of our listening model, represents the capacity to open your mind to others's views, and build upon these views in constructive ways.

3. Listen Emotionally

This is the highest level of listening. That's because it involves empathy, caring, and a desire to give support. Helen Keller learned that "The best and most beautiful things in the world cannot be seen nor even touched, but just felt in the heart."[4]

Emotional listening involves a range of qualities: politeness, political intelligence, an awareness of verbal and nonverbal cues, and a willingness to make the exchange enjoyable. Communication— including listening—should not only inspire action but also build relationships. Indeed, the two go together. The best listening is based on empathetic ties between the speaker and listener.

Politeness lays the groundwork for emotional listening. If you get angry, you'll close down lines of communication. The other person will react to your tone rather than your substance. Anger surfaces often enough in organizations, particularly where power relations are involved. It's a way of stating (often unconsciously) that "I don't want to hear what you have to tell me. I'm not interested in your point of view." Both parties lose in those exchanges.

Politeness means affirming the other person's statement (when you can) and being slow to contradict their pronouncements (when you don't agree).

Politeness also means not interrupting unnecessarily. Few people are boorish enough to cut others off in the middle of a word, but people may wait until there's a pause and jump in. Female clients tell me they experience this "voice-over" from colleagues. As a result, they're reluctant to pause. Even more disturbing is the tendency for others to jump in and complete a sentence for the speaker. These patterns of interruption undermine our ability to grasp what others mean.

There are, of course, times when a leader must step in and move the discussion forward. A room full of people will be grateful to be spared 90 minutes of rambling talk. The leader can say, "We're pressed for time. I can see you have a lot of good material here, but let's move to the home stretch."

Emotional listening goes beyond politeness—as important as that quality is. It involves a deeper sensitivity to the other person's feelings. Keep in mind the words of Helen Keller. The best listening is empathetic—it involves listening to the other person with your heart.

One of the most important ways to listen empathetically is to show respect. No manager is going to come out and say to you, "Give me respect." But everyone wants that recognition. Telling an executive assistant that she is "the best assistant in this company" may go a long way toward building her confidence and enabling her to tackle a still more challenging task. Showing respect to one's superiors is also critical. No one wants to come across as a sycophant, but one should not attack or "take on" a boss in a way that undermines his sense of worth.

An empathetic leader listens carefully both to the verbal and nonverbal responses of individuals. When you make a suggestion, be sensitive to the reaction of the person you're addressing. If their body language or words show they're put off by what you're saying, you must somehow address that problem.

Giving the other person a good deal of emotional "space" is another important part of being an empathetic listener. Imagine a circle. How much of the space is taken up by you, your ideas, your feelings? How much is taken up by the other person? People with a strong desire to manage or control take up more than half of the space. Effective listeners take up less than half. They respect the other person's "space." And they gain.

Emotional listening also involves making the exchange enjoyable for the other person. In most business conversations there is an opportunity to lighten up, share something funny or personal, and provide observations about life—children, sports, and other relevant topics. Take advantage of those moments and enjoy them. They'll make it easier for everyone to focus on the more serious material.

Listening skills provide a strong foundation for the steps that follow in this book. So if you want to lead, learn how to be an effective listener by mastering this three-tiered process. Good listening is physical, mental, and emotional, and, increasingly, it takes place on a much larger and often digital stage. As Harvard University president Drew Gilpin Faust states: "I spend a huge amount of time reaching out to people, either literally or digitally—all over the world. Leadership by walking around—that's a digital space now, it's virtual space."[5] Staying in touch with your audiences, showing them that you are reaching out and listening, will encourage them to listen to you.

CHAPTER 7

COMMIT TO COMMUNICATING

Often when we talk about great leaders and brilliant speakers, we describe them as if they won the genetic lottery. We say "He's a natural speaker." or "She's a born leader." We believe these influential individuals are born with extraordinary ability.

But in doing so, we ignore the commitment that these people have made to *becoming* good communicators. Yes, the best speakers make it look easy, but often their skill emerged only after much hard work. Many people know that Winston Churchill was a powerful orator. What few know is that, as a young man, he stuttered and had a lisp. And he collapsed from anxiety during his second address to the House of Commons![1] Churchill spent countless hours developing his "natural" leadership.

This chapter is all about commitment. To be sure, being committed to crafting and delivering a speech, a presentation, or impromptu remarks is no guarantee of success. If it were, this would be the only chapter in the book. But without commitment, the other guidelines in this book are at best halfway measures. If you want to be a great leader, the tools are within your grasp (in fact, they're in your hands right now), but you will have to *work* to master them. Here's what you can do:

- Follow the example of the greats—commit to improvement.
- Devote the time needed to create a powerful script.
- Practice your delivery (and practice again).

Follow the Example of the Greats—Commit to Improvement

Throughout history there have been individuals who stand out as remarkable speakers because of their extraordinary commitment. A concern with speaking better goes back at least to the time of the Bible. In Exodus we learn that Moses described himself as "slow of speech and slow of tongue."[2] He was concerned that when he appeared before Pharaoh he wouldn't be able to make his case effectively. But he improved with practice and with coaching from his brother, Aaron. Later in the Bible, Moses was celebrated as a "man of power in words and deeds."[3]

Similar concerns were evident among the ancient Greeks, who highly valued oratory. Demosthenes is known as one of the greatest speakers of all time, but he, too, was no natural. He retreated to a place underground and would go there for two to three months at a time. There he would exercise his voice and study the speeches of his day. To ensure that he wouldn't be tempted to come out, he shaved one side of his head. After emerging from the cave, he put pebbles in his mouth and spoke above the ocean's roar, so he could articulate more clearly.[4]

Abraham Lincoln, when he first spoke in public, was nervous and didn't know what to do with his hands. His voice seemed—both to himself and others—high-pitched and harsh. But he studied the best orators before becoming one himself. He rehearsed his major speeches before friends and colleagues.[5]

Bill Clinton, one of the best speakers among modern presidents, was also obsessive in his preparation. Every one of his major speeches reflected countless hours of planning and innumerable last-minute changes. He would receive drafts from his speechwriters—but that was only a beginning. For his first State of the Union Address, Clinton continually drafted and re-drafted the address. There was a 6:30 version, a 7:30 version, and an 8:30 version. The speech was to be delivered at 9 p.m. When Clinton began his delivery, the frantic teleprompter operator was desperately trying to make sure he had the latest version.[6]

In the corporate world, Apple's former CEO Steve Jobs will long be remembered as a charismatic speaker. But it didn't come naturally to him, either. Carmine Gallo, in his book *The Presentation Secrets of Steve Jobs*, tells us that "Steve Jobs is an extraordinary presenter because he works at it." His presentations improved steadily, from the time he introduced the Macintosh in 1984 to his wonderful Macworld talks in 2007 and after.[7]

Devote the Time Needed to Create a Powerful Script

The best speakers set aside the time needed to prepare a powerful script. If communicating is important to you—and it should be— carefully craft your remarks. That means devoting the necessary time whether you are delivering a formal speech, creating a presentation, or preparing for a Q&A session.

The need for preparation may seem most obvious when it comes to formal speeches. Nonetheless, I've seen executives take this task too lightly. In some cases they wing it, or jot a few notes down on the way to the podium. I don't advise such a cavalier approach.

In other cases, executives delegate the task of speech preparation without realizing the seriousness of this process. When I was a corporate speechwriter, I had access to most of the CEOs I wrote for. But many speechwriters find that their top executives are closely guarded. They tell me they often receive directives from two or three removes. In bureaucratic organizations the speechwriter might be five removes from the executive client. No wonder speeches often sound generic and less forceful than they might be.

The better approach? If you have to give a speech or make a presentation, follow in the footsteps of the great leaders and put in the hours needed to make your talk inspirational. If you are working with a speechwriter or assistant, brief them personally. Direct them well, and make clear what messages are important to you.

Below the top echelon, most executives and managers prepare their own talks. When creating a presentation, particularly a PowerPoint talk with slides, it's all too easy to assemble a set of visuals and talk from them. Unfortunately, that path will lead only to an information dump and a boring, forgettable talk. Instead, create a script first, and only then build the slides to reflect the message in the script. If you don't like reading from a full script, pare it back to talking points and speak from them. It may seem to be a longer process to first create a script, then visuals, then talking points. But this process will serve you best.

Preparation is no less important for informal and off-the-cuff occasions, such as phone calls or Q&As. Here are ways you can make sure you prepare for those exchanges.

- If you're planning a meeting with employees, analysts, or management, make a list of the likely issues that will be raised. Take a leaf from presidential campaigns where candidates take off several days to prepare for debates. You won't need that much time, but you might book off the afternoon and have your staff pepper you with probable questions. Get your messages right. It could make a significant difference in employee relations or share value.

- Before an important phone call, take a few minutes to jot down notes. By choosing your words carefully, you'll deliver the right leadership messages, and avoid hanging up the phone thinking, "I should not have said that!"

- Develop an "elevator script" that inspires others about your product or your business, so when you are in a meeting, on the golf course—or in the elevator—you can spread the word.

- Write a short script about yourself that you can draw upon when you want to lead and influence. For example, if you are an HR manager and see the president of your company in a chance encounter, instead of blurting out whatever comes into your mind, you can say: "Hello, I'm Jess Ziegler. I lead the group that develops our firm's top talent."

Practice Your Delivery (and Practice Again)

Commitment also extends to rehearsing your remarks. The last section of this book, "Achieve a Leader's Presence," goes into detail about *how* to speak effectively. But knowing the proper techniques is not enough—you must practice. As this chapter suggests, a sustained, strong commitment to speaking well has characterized the best orators in history. When I poll executives and managers, I often find that they spend even less time rehearsing a presentation or talk than they do writing it. They often don't think about the pauses, the drama, or the "shape" of their remarks, when, in fact, every script has those attributes. In every paragraph, on every page, some statements are far more important than others. If you are not aware of these emphases, your audience won't be, either. Rehearsing allows you to develop that necessary deep understanding of your script. Here are several ways to rehearse your talk.

- **Read it out loud to yourself, again and again.** This will get you comfortable with the text, and with the rhythm of the ideas. Underline key words and phrases. And, if you repeatedly stumble over any turn of phrase, get rid of it.
- **Read it in front of your children.** They will be good at telling you whether you sound real!
- **Read it in front of a speech coach.** You will learn how to bring the script to life by achieving the appropriate tone, pace, expression, and body language.

The Humphrey Group rehearses clients for important events, and the results can be transformational. I once worked with a vice president who was dreading the fact that he had to give a two-minute speech to the senior executives in his company. This is an audience that can be very critical. Normally, in such situations, people just live with their nerves and don't rehearse because they are too scared to do so. But he was in a coaching program with me, and he used the opportunity to prepare. Initially, when he delivered his talk, he mumbled the words and assumed a defensive posture: head down, eyes unfocused, arms closed, and he spoke in a tight, clipped tone. But as we worked together over several hours, I encouraged him to connect with the text, emphasizing important words and showing ownership of key statements. As he did so, his eyes became more focused. He unclenched his hands and began to speak with conviction. Little by little he developed a more genuine, expressive presence. All of this resulted in a superior performance that made the rehearsal well worth the time and effort!

Whatever else you learn from this book, commitment is crucial for your success. See "A Story of Commitment" below. This true story is about Linda Stromme, who became one of the best speakers in her company, Bank of Montreal Financial Group, and rose to the position of Assistant Chief Auditor. Her story not only shows the importance of commitment, but also provides a prelude to the remaining chapters of this book, which will take you on a similar journey. Indeed, it is the same journey all great speakers take. Few of the most famous orators were "naturals"—they worked hard to develop this skill.

A Story of Commitment

by Linda Stromme

I feared public speaking more than anything. In my first job in an accounting firm I stumbled my way through presentations. Thankfully expectations were low—if we presented the right numbers, that was enough. Then I joined a large bank where the need to speak well was critical. In my first month my new boss held a large meeting and asked each member of his executive team to lead part of the meeting. I went into panic mode and I'm still not really sure what I said. It must have been pretty bad since my boss sent the video of my presentation to The Humphrey Group and told them to help me out.

I was relieved that someone was going to provide me with one-on-one coaching, and was greeted by a warm executive speech coach. After going through my presentation, he asked me, "What is your message?" Wow, I need to have a message? No one had ever mentioned that before. I also discovered a framework for designing scripts. The content and clarity of my presentations improved dramatically.

I then needed to work on my delivery, so I bravely volunteered to report on a project to the vice chairman and his direct reports. I knew this would give me an opportunity to strengthen my delivery style. My colleagues were thrilled that I volunteered—they were off the hook! My coach showed me how to make my body language more powerful using large, more confident gestures. I also learned how to stop my nervous movements and assume a more stable stance at the podium. Voice work was also part of the coaching, and I discovered how to project my voice using diaphragmatic breathing. My coach also told me how to emphasize certain words and phrases to better convey my message.

We rehearsed the presentation at least 10 times and I felt very comfortable. While I was very prepared for this presentation, my nerves still got the better of me on the morning of the meeting. Fortunately, my actor/coach in The Humphrey Group pointed out that all actors and speakers are nervous before they start a performance or presentation, and without nerves the delivery would be very dull and flat. I now worry if I don't feel some nervous tension before a presentation.

I got to the room and was surprised to find that I would be confined to a small area, as I had to speak into a microphone for an international caller. I couldn't walk around as much as I had in my rehearsal. At first this threw me off, but I was so well prepared that the presentation came off without a hitch. On my way out of the room, the head of human resources asked me to join her for lunch and said she needed to get to know me better. One very senior executive who was usually critical said: "You are pretty smooth at the podium." Coming from him I knew I had nailed the speech.

I was proud of my hard-won accomplishment and realized I had become a strong speaker. This was all because I had made a decision to be a better, stronger, and more polished speaker. The journey was not difficult—it just took tons of commitment.

STEP 2

SCRIPT YOURSELF AS A LEADER

- ◆ What Is a Leader's Script?
- ◆ Open with a Grabber
- ◆ State Your Subject
- ◆ Lead with a Message
- ◆ Develop a Persuasive Structure
- ◆ Close with a Call to Action

CHAPTER 8

WHAT IS A LEADER'S SCRIPT?

"*The time has come,*" *the Walrus said,*
"*To talk of many things:*
Of shoes—and ships—and sealing wax—
Of cabbages—and kings—
And why the sea is boiling hot—
And whether pigs have wings."[1]
　　—Lewis Carroll, *Through the Looking-Glass*

The Walrus rambled on and on, skipping from topic to topic. That approach was fine for him and his friend the Carpenter: they didn't expect their audience, the oysters, to live to hear the end of their remarks. But your expectations must be different. You want to keep your audience and win them over. You want to convince them that your message is important. You want them to act upon your recommendations. To achieve these goals you must be focused and well organized. You must have what this work calls The Leader's Script™.

The Leader's Script lies at the heart of this section of the book and is described in the next five chapters. Follow this approach, and you'll shape your raw material—your information, ideas, and data—into a powerful talk that inspires others.

The Power of The Leader's Script

The Leader's Script is a template for designing your remarks— whether you are speaking for 30 minutes or 30 seconds. It has extraordinary versatility and strength. This single model works when giving a formal speech or a presentation, responding to questions, speaking on the phone, or having a brief conversation with a colleague. You need only this one design for your scripts. You need to master only one methodology for all situations. By using this template you will always be "on message" and will influence and inspire others.

The Leader's Script has been created, thoroughly tested, and refined by The Humphrey Group in our work with thousands of clients. It reflects the practices of the very best speakers, and it works around the globe. We have coached countless leaders whose approach to communicating has been transformed by this template.

Most significantly, The Leader's Script is more than a model for clear speaking. It is a strategy for sound thinking and reasoning. It will make you more persuasive in every situation. It will enable you to lead every time you speak.

The Elements of The Leader's Script

Let's look at the three parts of this scripting template. They are the Introduction, Body, and Conclusion.

1. The Introduction

A good Introduction draws the audience in and aligns them with your thinking. It transforms listeners from people sitting in a room, to a group that's interested in what you are about to say. In short, it sets you up for success.

The Introduction has four components: the grabber, the subject, the message, and a structural statement. For a formal speech or presentation, you will want all four components, but for a comment at a meeting, you won't need to state your subject, because it will be obvious from the discussion. In this case, you'll have only three elements in your opening: grabber, message, and structural statement. And in a telephone call, you might only have two of these four parts: a brief grabber and a message, moving on to the body of your remarks. But think of all four elements as important for most scripts.

Here's an overview of the four components of the Introduction. (Chapters 9, 10, and 11 look at these elements in greater detail.)

- The *grabber* is your opening: it captures the audience's attention. In a formal speech, the opening can be an anecdote or story. In informal remarks, the grabber might simply be a warm greeting to the audience or a segue from what another person has said.
- The *subject*, which follows the grabber, presents the topic. It tells the audience what you'll be talking about. It begins with expressions

like "I'd like to look at . . ." or "The presentation will review . . ." or "I called you to discuss . . ."

- Next comes the *message*, which sets forth your argument. The message represents the essence of your thinking and is the most important statement in your talk. As a leader you must believe in your message, and your goal must be to get the audience to believe in it, too. Always express it in a single sentence.

- The Introduction often ends with a *structural statement*. It follows the message, and tells your audience how you'll be making your case. You might state, "I say that for three reasons," or "I'll first discuss the challenge, then I'll outline our response." Think of it as a roadmap for the body of your talk.

2. The Body

The Body of your script contains the arguments that develop your main message and should be organized in a clear structure. For example, in a phone call you might discuss the three reasons why your product will benefit a client's company. Or if you're talking to your boss in that one-minute elevator ride, you might say, "Here's the challenge we're facing." And then a few moments later, "This is the solution we've come up with." However long your script, organize the Body around a logical pattern. (This will be described in chapter 12.)

3. The Conclusion

Your script ends with a Conclusion, which contains two elements: the restated message and the call to action.

- The *restated message* brings your audience back to your central idea. In restating it, make them feel that they now own the message. For example, you might say, "So you can see why I say that we are on course to deliver a great performance."

- The *call to action* is the final element. It outlines the steps to be taken in response to your message. (Chapter 13 discusses the call to action more fully.)

The Leader's Script is a template that ensures you will lead whenever you speak. The next page presents a diagram of this model. Using this model, you will have a clear message, develop it persuasively, and ask the audience to act upon it. Will you always deliver the script uninterrupted? No. In an off-the-cuff meeting, the flow of dialogue may mean you get to your message, but not immediately to the supporting arguments. But if you keep your script in mind, you will eventually move through all your proof points and to the conclusion. Every time you use The Leader's Script you will come across as an influential individual. This template will help transform your audience into followers, and your speaking into an act of leadership. So, burn it in your mind. Use it for thinking and for speaking. Put The Leader's Script at the core of everything you communicate.

The Leader's Script™

Grabber: _____

Subject: _____

Message: _____

Structural
Statement: _____

The following points prove the message. They are organized around one of five patterns: "Reasons," "Ways," "Situation and Response," "Present Results and Future Prospects," and "Chronological."

Point One: _____

       A: _____

       B: _____

       C: _____

Point Two: _____

       A: _____

       B: _____

       C: _____

Point Three: _____

       A: _____

       B: _____

       C: _____

Restated Message: _____

Call to Action: _____

CHAPTER 9

OPEN WITH A GRABBER

The American minister Henry Ward Beecher had a gift for speaking. One July morning he rode into a West Virginia town known as "Death Valley" because the townsfolk were such a deadly audience for any speaker. By the time Beecher was introduced, half the audience was asleep. Undaunted, Beecher rose from his chair and, wiping his brow, strode to the front of the platform.

"It's a God-damned hot day," the clergyman began.

A thousand pairs of eyes stared in shock. Beecher paused and then, raising a finger of reproof, went on, "That's what I heard a man say here this afternoon!"

He then delivered a stirring condemnation of blasphemy—and took the audience with him.[1]

Not every speaker should begin so dramatically, but your opening is important. It's the first component of The Leader's Script, and your first opportunity to engage your audience. Get it right and you'll be well on your way to making your case.

The Role of the Grabber

The grabber plays a crucial role in The Leader's Script. It draws the audience in and leads them to your message. Why bother reaching out to an audience, especially when time is short, or when the people in the room (or the single person you're talking to) are familiar? The answer is that a good opening makes your listeners far more receptive to you and your message.

When you address a colleague or walk up to a podium, your audience may well have their thoughts elsewhere. They may be reflecting on problems they've been wrestling with all morning, or thinking about the next meeting they'll be attending or the vacation they're about to take. Just think of it, when you begin speaking you may have bodies in the room that *look* like an audience, but their minds are often elsewhere. In these situations, plunging directly into your subject is like pushing your audience into a cold lake: it's an unpleasant shock to the system. Audiences need to be transformed from people just sitting there to people who are eager to hear what you have to say.

Every grabber also has a second role: it provides a transition to your message. If you begin your remarks with a story that has little relationship to your larger point, the audience may be briefly engaged, but they'll soon wonder about the point of your opening. You will have squandered the opportunity to move smoothly toward your argument.

Grabbers are important in both informal and formal situations. In informal situations they serve as a bridge to your audience—a way into the conversation you want to have. In formal situations, they help overcome the distance between you and your audience—distance created by the size of the room, the presence of the podium or stage, the formality of the event, or your own jitters.

Creating a Grabber

How should you create a grabber? You have two broad options. The opening can be personal or literary. Let's look at each in turn.

The Personal Grabber

Personal grabbers are like a verbal handshake. You can't reach out personally to every member of the audience, but you can "shake hands" with your audience verbally in one of three ways: (1) sharing something about yourself, (2) sharing something you know about your audience, or (3) discussing a common bond between you and the audience. These are, respectively, the "I," "you," and "we" grabbers.

The "I" grabber creates a connection by revealing something about you. For example:

- A young vice president finds herself in the cafeteria line just ahead of her CEO. She begins: "I've just been on the leadership retreat that you funded, and I found it exceptionally valuable." The CEO is delighted.

- A team leader for a project begins his status report to his boss by saying, "I am excited about this project, and my team has devoted long hours to its success." This positive "I" opening successfully frames his update.

- Benazir Bhutto used the "I" grabber to great effect in the opening of her 2007 speech on Islam, introducing personal elements like her family and her heritage:

> I stand before you not only as the first female Prime Minister of my nation and the leader of the opposition, but also as a woman, a wife, and a mother. I stand before you as a woman proud of my cultural and religious heritage. I want to use this opportunity, speaking to many of you here today who are not Muslims, to tell you about the Islam I was taught. Islam taught me that men and women are equal in the eyes of God. It is this message of Islam that has empowered me, has strengthened me, and has emboldened me.[2]

Avoid "I" grabbers that are vague or platitudinous ("I'm pleased to be here. It's always nice to address your organization . . .") or self-deprecating ("Good afternoon. I'm the new controller, and I've only been here for two months, so I'm just learning myself . . ."). Language such as this does not position you as a leader.

The "you" grabber shows empathy, appreciation, understanding, or gratitude toward your audience. For example:

- A team leader talking to his employees might open with empathy: "All of you have been under great pressure during these last months . . ."
- A company president could begin a Town Hall meeting with appreciation: "It has taken all of you—home office, field, sales, support functions, and corporate—working together to achieve the results you have just seen on this video."
- A project manager might show understanding of his boss's position before providing a countervailing point of view: "I understand what you've been looking for from us."

- Morgan Freeman, accepting his Oscar for best supporting actor in *Million Dollar Baby*, began with gratitude: "I want to thank everybody and anybody who ever had anything at all to do with the making of this picture. But I especially want to thank Clint Eastwood for giving me the opportunity to work with him again."[3]

Avoid "you" grabbers that begin with "You're wrong," "I disagree," or "I was disappointed with your work." They create tension and undercut your leadership.

The "we" grabber builds rapport with a team and helps develop consensus in the room. For example:

- A team leader recognizes the work of his team, saying, "Good afternoon. When we took on this project we had no idea what its scope would be—what we were actually getting into, and how many nights we'd be leaving the office at 2 a.m. Nor did we imagine what huge gains we could make in the productivity of this division. All of us are here today to celebrate our success."
- An individual at a meeting uses the "we" grabber to build consensus: "Our discussion has been going in a number of directions. But we do have consensus in several areas."

Avoid using "we" in a vague or "royal" sense. If you begin, "We've had remarkable accomplishments this year," make sure people know who "we" is.

These personal grabbers—"I," "you," and "we"—all draw the speaker and audience together, and create a bond that gives the speaker a receptive audience.

The Literary Grabber

You can also use grabbers from published or "literary" sources. While these may be used in everyday scripts, they are more commonly reserved for formal speeches and presentations. Literary grabbers come in many forms.

- **Anecdotes, proverbs, and humor** can provide a rich source for your openings, and books of anecdotes and proverbs are abundant. But use them with care. Make sure any stories you use lead into your message, and avoid stories that are overused, sexist, or offensive. Humor must be treated with a "Handle with Care" sign, as discussed in chapter 21.

- **Quotations** can set the stage for your message in both formal and everyday remarks. For example, an investment manager might begin a presentation to her team by saying: "The *Wall Street Journal* last week had an article entitled 'You Snooze, You Lose.' The article focused on the fast-paced world of international currency trading, but the message is just as relevant for us as it is for global money managers. We, too, must be vigilant in managing our customers' portfolios in these volatile times. If we snooze, not only do we lose, but our customers lose. And we can't let that happen."

  Quotations can also be used effectively in formal speeches. Here's a university president quoting Winston Churchill: "'The Empires of the future are the Empires of the mind.'[4] These words, spoken by Winston Churchill more than a half century ago, describe the reality we now face. We live in a knowledge society. Our minds will shape our future. And higher education will play a critical role in developing the next generation of thinkers. But universities and colleges alone cannot meet the demands of our knowledge-based society. Tonight I'd like to suggest that all of us must work together—universities, governments, businesses, communities, and families—to build a society in which strong minds shape our future."

- **Statistics** can also provide a provocative opening. The head of an IT department began a PowerPoint presentation by displaying the number 111,000,000 on the screen. He let it sit there for a moment, then said, "That's the number of spam messages sent every day to mobile phones and computers around the world. And since it's just after 8 p.m., we're rapidly approaching that number today. I'm here to talk about our anti-spam capabilities. I believe that our anti-spam efforts are crucial to improving customer satisfaction."

- **Research** grabs your audience's attention by telling them something they've never heard before. One of my favorite grabbers was delivered by David Galloway, then President and CEO of Torstar Corporation, a firm that owns Harlequin Enterprises Ltd, a publisher of romance novels. He addressed a distinguished audience at the Harvard Business School Club with the following opening.

"How many of you have read one of our romance novels? Put up your hand if you have." [David walked to center stage and put his own hand up. But there was silence in the audience.]

"Well, you should," the speaker continued. "I'll tell you something about our readers. They read more books than other people do . . . and they have better sex lives."

Still holding his hand up, David said "I guess you will have to take my word for it."

The audience laughed and then a lone voice from the back of the room shouted out: "How many books does it take?" The room was engaged!

- **Short videos** can create a powerful opening. When physicist Stephen Hawking spoke at the White House, he began with a video clip adapted from the television series *Star Trek: The Next Generation*.[5] In the clip Hawking, Sir Isaac Newton, and Albert Einstein are playing poker with the show's android character. Hawking wins the game! He then moves from that grabber to his own vision of the distant future and why his vision will prevail over the other interpretations.

- **Poetic openings** work wonders, too. Try writing your own poetry, as was done by one of our clients, Ginny Dybenko, President, Bell Advanced Communications. She introduced her speech on broadband technology with the following words:

> Gather round friends and I'll tell you a tale
> About an opportunity sweeping the land.
> It will strengthen relationships and add to your sales.
> And the name of this magic is Broadband.
>
> It speeds multimedia, and makes possible solutions
> Before customer demands get out of hand.
> In fact, you'd be hard pressed to find institutions
> That aren't planning a shift to Broadband.
>
> So, colleagues gathered here, I've begun with a Tale
> About this opportunity sweeping our Land.

With your help we'll go forward, with sale after sale
And we'll corner the market for Broadband.

Who said business doesn't have its lyrical moments?

Grabbers, which can be personal or literary, are the first component of The Leader's Script. The Roman poet Horace said, "He who has begun has half done."[6] With a good grabber, you have engaged your audience, and have drawn them to your message. You are well on your way to persuading them.

CHAPTER 10

STATE YOUR SUBJECT

Every talk has a subject. Get it wrong and you're in trouble. That happened at a dinner given in honor of the sports and communications magnate Ted Turner. The people in the audience were highflyers from Toronto's media elite. When it came time for the speeches, there was a big buildup to Turner. He walked to the podium and began with pleasantries: "It's great to be here in what I'd call better times. Last time I was here the Toronto Blue Jays beat my Atlanta Braves. Tonight is a much happier occasion." Then there was a pause, Turner thought for a moment and, turning to the host, said, "What the hell did you want me to talk about anyway?" Ted Turner's question may have been funny, but his lack of a subject must have taken the audience aback.

Determining Your Subject

The subject defines what you will be talking about, so it's critical to get it right. You cannot have a strong leadership script unless you are invested in your subject.

1. Carefully Choose or Redefine Your Subject

Invitations to speak often come with words like "We would like you to speak about nuclear power: its pros and cons." Well, if you are from the nuclear industry you will not want a "pros and cons" approach. You will want to focus on the benefits of nuclear power. So don't fall into the trap of deferring to those who invited you by designing your talk around *their* views.

Occasionally, speaking requests go well beyond your area of expertise or provide a topic that's too broad. Narrow the topic so that it reflects your expertise. For example, suppose the Rotary Club has asked you to talk on banking. If you're a small business lender, and your audience is financial planners, narrow the subject to "How banks can help small business." The same holds true for other communication situations. If someone asks you a question that's too broad to answer, such as "What is the Red Cross doing for developing countries?" narrow the subject by responding: "We have a broad range of initiatives for helping developing countries, but let me tell you about one I was recently involved in myself: reuniting families that were separated by the conflict in Libya."

2. Bring Excitement to Your Subject

Some clients tell us that their subject is boring. If your subject seems dull, replace it with a topic that will more fully energize your audience (and you!). For example, instead of speaking on auditing practices for government agencies, recast it as "CSI Comes to Washington." A presentation on active currency management might become "Making Money with Money."

3. Focus on One Subject

Often speakers discuss multiple subjects. For example, a speaker might say, "There are four things I want to talk about today." Or a keynote speaker might begin, "Well, good morning. I'm going to talk about our company, its place in global markets, why our customers come to us, and what we are doing to keep their faith." Already the speaker is on the road to an information dump. You need a single subject if you are going to have a single, powerful message.

Announcing Your Subject

Announce your subject immediately following the grabber. In a formal speech the subject might be stated as follows: "Today I will look at the impact of social media on companies in our industry." If you are leading a meeting, your subject might sound like this: "Today we will discuss how we can better manage the work flow for our team."

Leading into your subject is an art. It needs to be smooth. In the above-mentioned meeting example you might move from grabber to subject in this way: "Thanks for coming. I'm delighted to have the entire team with us. Being together allows us to talk about a subject that's near and dear to our hearts: better managing the work flow for our team."

If yours is a difficult topic, you may even want to lead into your subject with a sense of humor.

Grabber: I know the very notion of mathematical modeling can be
daunting, especially when delivered by a Ph.D. But there
is a method in my madness.

Subject: I want to give you an opportunity to see how our mathematical models can create value for you, our M&A specialists.

A subject defines the content of your remarks. It's an important
element of The Leader's Script. You want your topic to be unmistakable, so announce it with the following words:

"I will discuss . . ."

"I will look at . . ."

"Let's focus on . . ."

"Let me tell you about . . ."

In a few situations you don't need a subject statement. For example,
in a meeting those present know what the subject is, so you can move
directly from your grabber to your message.

Grabber: That's an issue we take very seriously.

Message: In fact, our company has demonstrated our deep respect
for the environment.

A subject matters. It defines your focus and lays the groundwork
for your message. It plays an important role in guiding your audience
to your argument.

CHAPTER 11

LEAD WITH A MESSAGE

Too many people ramble on, like Toad in *The Wind in the Willows*. The animals didn't want him to speak or even sing, and Rat tells him why:

> "Look here, Toad," Rat said one day. "It's about this Banquet, and very sorry I am to have to speak to you like this. But we want you to understand clearly, once and for all, that there are going to be no speeches and no songs."
>
> "Just one little song," Toad pleaded.
>
> "It's no good, Toady," Rat replied. "You know well that your songs are all conceit and boasting."
>
> "And gas," put in the Badger.[1]

Speakers like Toad leave their audiences with no message. Listeners feel the presenter has nothing to say—only "gas." Information is presented, but to no apparent end. Such speakers lack a distinct point of view. Every talk must have a clearly stated message. It's the heart of your talk. It's the argument that engages the audience and presents your point of view.

Why the Message Is So Important

For many of our clients the single most important "take away" from our training is that they should have a message every time they speak. It seems simple, but it's an extraordinarily powerful insight. Almost by itself, a strong, clear message moves you from "information" to "inspiration." It tells your audience why they are in the room. Without a message you cannot lead.

I worked with a senior executive who came to me because her entire strategy group had been disbanded. The problem was that she had gone on a cross-country tour of her company's offices to sell a new strategy. She did significant damage because she could not clearly explain why the company was committed to a particular vision. *She had no message.* She was smart and knowledgeable. But she got so embedded in the information that she could not get across a simple, straightforward message about the strategy. And without a message, one loses control of the audience's response. She told me that people in her audience got angry at her because they didn't see why such major changes were being undertaken. She didn't get the buy-in she was hoping for and within a year her group was disbanded.

The message is often the "missing link" in informal exchanges, too. When we speak off-the-cuff our thoughts can tumble out of our minds in no particular order and often without any clear perspective. Take the following example of a new CEO who was on a conference call with his senior employees. He spoke without notes, and what spilled out of his mind were his unfiltered and deep concerns about the future of the company and what the media was saying about it.

> Good afternoon. I'll be brief. I can tell you we are not in financial trouble. We have a great national network. There is speculation that we are going to sell the company. The company was in financial trouble before . . . so there's nothing new here. We have to stop worrying about what's in the media. All of you, and those who report to you, must focus on your day-to-day jobs.

By saying whatever was on his mind, he delivered many messages willy-nilly, and several were damaging. Saying "We are not in financial trouble" was as good as saying "We *are* in financial trouble." Alluding to what was happening in the media clearly suggested that others were reporting bad news.

Even many leaders who are considered superb speakers have had to learn how to get control of what they say, and deliver a single clear, inspiring message. According to John Heilemann and Mark Halperin in their book *Game Change*, Barack Obama, during the first debates in the 2007 Democratic primary, "had a lot to say and wasn't good at spitting it out quickly or concisely, tending to back into his responses. Rather than sell one idea well, he tried to squeeze in as many points as possible. 'I have sixty seconds,' he said in prep, 'How much do you guys think I can get into sixty seconds?'" When his chief strategist, David Axelrod, showed him the video of the debates, Obama grimaced. "*It's worse than I thought* ran through his mind. He pledged to do better."[2] After that, Obama learned the power of speaking with one message. His speeches, press conferences, and informal remarks all improved.

Your message is the single most important element of your script. Don't leave your audience wondering where you are heading. Former U.S. president Dwight Eisenhower once looked at a talk his speechwriter had given him, and demanded, "What is the QED?" Then, seeing the puzzled look on the face of his writer, he explained, "QED—*quod erat demonstrandum*. What's the bottom line? What is the message you want the audience to take away with them?"[3] Similarly, according to author James Humes, "Churchill suggested writing out the bottom line first. Write out in one sentence—before you start preparing your remarks—the message you want to leave with your listeners."[4]

The script's message governs everything else you say. Aristotle, the father of rhetoric, wrote in his famous treatise, *Poetics*, that a plot should have a unity of purpose.[5] He argued that every element of the plot should relate to every other element, developing one unified theme. The same is true for speeches and informal remarks. Everything in a speech or talk should relate back to one clear message. The message is at the heart of The Leader's Script. It is the most important part of the template. Get it right and you're well on your way to becoming an influential speaker. Get it wrong, and everything else you do will not make up for its omission.

Placement of Your Message

The message is the linchpin of your script: state it in the beginning, prove it in the body, and come back to it at the end.

If you only have one sentence, it should be your message. Sergey Brin, co-founder of Google, sent the following one-sentence tweet: "Haiti relief mission: they need as much help as they can get."[6]

While your message appears in the Introduction, it is rarely the first sentence. Imagine beginning a phone call or a meeting with the words: "My point is we need to move forward with this project with greater speed." That would be too abrupt. You need to focus the audience's attention first. That's why your script typically opens with a grabber followed by a subject, as in the example below that captures the words of an employer interviewing a candidate for a position:

Grabber: Thank you for coming in to talk with us. You have strong credentials, but there must be a good fit, too.

Subject: So let me tell you about what we look for in employees.

Message: Quite simply, if you want to work for our advertising firm, you need some mojo, some color, and enormous passion for the business.

When presenting your message, be bold. Make sure your audience hears this sentence as your key message. Some common ways of leading into your message are the following:

"My message is . . ."

"If there is one idea I want you to leave with today, it is that . . ."

"I believe that . . ."

"My point is that . . ."

"As I see it . . ."

"Quite simply . . ."

In the list above, the first two ways of framing your message would apply to formal talks, the last four to less formal situations.

Come back to your message at the beginning of your Conclusion. Having proven it in the body of your script, you can now assume that your audience is "on side." For example, you might say, "So you can see why I feel so strongly that . . ." Or simply reaffirm your message: "Let me emphasize, my message this afternoon has been . . ."

Creating Your Message

Every message should embody five characteristics.

1. **It must be stated in one short sentence.** For any idea to be clear, it must be captured in a single, easy-to-grasp sentence. A sentence is a unit of meaning. Two sentences are two ideas. And a run-on sentence is several ideas thrown together. So, keep it simple, and state your message in one succinct sentence that can be remembered. You may not be as brief as, "I have a dream," but still your sentence should be clear and well-focused.

2. **It must engage your audience.** Here is where listening to your audience becomes so important. You must reach their hearts and minds with your message. Avoid platitudes and self-evident statements. If you are addressing a sales meeting, and you state: "My message is that we must do better next year," be prepared for shrugs. But if you say, "My point is that we're going to give you the tools to work smarter and grow your sales in the coming year," you'll capture their attention.

3. **It must fit with your organization's outlook.** Every business presentation is a corporate statement. For that reason your message should be positive and inspire belief in your company or organization. Strong, positive corporate messages must be delivered not only by the CEO but also by leaders at all levels. Your role is to create believers in your organization.

4. **It must reflect your convictions.** Your message should be an idea you fully embrace, and others must see and hear it as yours. So look at your message and say, "Are my convictions in it?" When those convictions are present, you'll find the language you use is strong and authentic.

5. **It must be well supported.** Your argument must be based on sound research and careful reasoning. Otherwise, your listeners will remain skeptical about your case, and you will have lost an opportunity to lead.

Write out your message and test it against these five criteria. Rework it if necessary. With a well-defined message, you're well on your way to a successful talk.

Different Messages for Different Talks

While speaking engagements vary greatly, you must always have a message, properly placed and properly developed. Clearly, you'll have more time to polish that message if you're presenting a formal speech than if you're involved in an elevator conversation.

A formal speech will have the elements of the Introduction most clearly and fully developed. You'll begin with a grabber, then state the subject, and finally the message. Here's one example:

Grabber (personal): When I began my first managerial position, there were few visible minorities in senior roles in this company. I was mistaken for a person in the maintenance department. Fortunately, that situation has changed over the past 10 years.

Subject: I want to talk to you today about Furlong Corporation's commitment to diversity.

Message: The message I want you to leave with is that Furlong has now put in place three vital programs that will help visible minorities advance in our company.

In a PowerPoint presentation the message should appear up front, usually on the second slide. The first slide often shows your subject, and most frequently the grabber is delivered while the subject slide is shown. Consider the following example:

Grabber (spoken while slide 1 is shown): Welcome to Investor Day. We're delighted to have you with us, and appreciate your keen interest in our company. As analysts who follow us, you help us get our story out to the investment community. We're now pleased to share the next chapter with you.

Slide 1, Subject slide: Auric Metals—Our Results, 2011

Speaker: Today I will give you an overview of our results for 2011.

Slide 2, Message slide: Excellent earnings from rising gold prices and soaring production.

Speaker: The message of my presentation is that we had an excellent year thanks to rising gold prices and soaring production at our three largest mines.

Imagine another situation: an elevator conversation. You're a manager who is sharing an elevator ride to the 59th floor with an executive vice president. There are just the two of you for this one-minute ride. You could stare at the wall or comment on the rainy weather—and so lose a rare opportunity to speak with your boss's boss. Instead, you seize the opportunity.

Grabber: Bob, let me introduce myself. I'm Raj Gopul, manager for private wealth banking.

Subject: I wanted to tell you the referrals we've received from your office have been excellent.

Message: Just in the past month we've doubled the list of clients who are investing between one and five million dollars with us.

When responding to questions in a Q&A session, you need to present a message with every reply. The question usually provides the subject—so you'll only need a grabber and message.

Question: Can you explain why the development of your pipeline is taking so long? After all, it's been over two years since you announced this initiative.

Grabber: At Rolland Oil we're committed to protecting the environment.

Message: So we've taken two years to make sure that we address all environmental issues related to the pipeline.

Even a tweet should have a leader's message. Bill Gates, head of the Gates Foundation, tweeted, "A world without Malaria? It's Possible."[7]

Note that in each case above, the message is a clear, forceful statement that tests well with all five criteria. The individual speaking is "on message" and projects the clarity of a leader.

Conclusion

Your message is the most important element of your script, and a good message will define you as a leader who has something to say—something your audience can believe in. To develop a strong sense of argument, ask yourself every time you speak, "What is my message?" Practice this discipline in both formal and impromptu situations, and you will get better and better at formulating clear, compelling messages. You will not only learn to *speak* with a message, you will also learn to *think* with a message. You will become a stronger, more dynamic leader who inspires others.

CHAPTER 12

DEVELOP A PERSUASIVE STRUCTURE

The White Rabbit put on his spectacles.

"Where shall I begin, please your Majesty?" he asked.

"Begin at the beginning," the King said very gravely, "and go on till you come to the end: then stop."[1]

— Lewis Carroll, *Alice's Adventures in Wonderland*

These lines provide a simple view of structure. But the King's words are not that far removed from Aristotle's suggestion that a good structure should be "a complete whole in itself, with a beginning, middle, and end . . . ."[2] Indeed, The Leader's Script has a beginning, middle, and end.

After your script's Introduction comes the Body, or middle. This chapter shows you how to structure the Body of your script so that you persuade your audience of your message.

The Pitfalls of Poor Structure

The Body of your talk should do one thing: prove your message. If you fail to structure your talk effectively, your audience will be unconvinced or bored, or will simply wonder what you are talking about. The well-crafted message statement you began with will be left high and dry. Unfortunately, poorly structured talks are all too common.

One flawed approach to building the Body of a script is *rambling*. This occurs when a speaker meanders from one topic to the next. The result is an information dump. Too often speakers take this tack when they are poorly prepared, overconfident (which often leads to being poorly prepared), or simply nervous. Sometimes they'll apologize, saying, "Sorry, I guess I'm rambling." Some straightforward advice: Avoid the apologies. Don't ramble.

Another poor approach to structure is what I'd call *pseudo-organization*. This method characterizes individuals who seem to have their material under control, but in fact present a series of disconnected lists. I remember sitting through such an address delivered by the CEO of a large insurance company. He began the body of his talk by explaining the "five forces changing the industry." Next he reviewed four strategies that had no clear relationship to the forces of change, and he concluded with the five things his company could do. These points, too, bore no connection to what had preceded them. I felt as if I was watching a building being put up where a different set of architects had designed each floor.

PowerPoint frequently fosters pseudo-organization. Overloaded slides with bulleted lists are too often the mainstay of these presentations. Everything seems to be organized. The graphics are impressive and colorful. But when you carefully analyze such talks, it's clear there is only the appearance of organization. Points do not line up. There is no logic to the presentation of evidence. It is no wonder that so many PowerPoint talks are Power*Pointless*.

The Basics of Sound Organization

Organizing your talk is not difficult if you put the effort into building a sound structure. Here are five guidelines to help you get the structure right.

1. Present Arguments, Not Topics

The Body of The Leader's Script should provide arguments that prove your message. No one will be convinced by a structure that simply lists topics. "Next point, spending on computers," sounds a lot less convincing than, "Next, we're going to give each of you a tablet PC so you can be more productive on sales calls." Whether you are organizing an answer to a question, a brief talk, a presentation, or a formal speech, make certain that each of your main points in the Body is a complete sentence and presents a sound argument in support of your main idea.

A good way to think about these organizing statements is to consider them as message statements for one portion of the talk. Just as you should never present a brief subject as your overall message, a topic cannot serve as an organizing statement.

Let's look at an outline of the Body of a well-structured script. What we see is a set of logically connected ideas or arguments, all of which must point back to and prove your message.

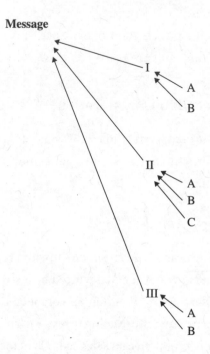

Note that the main ideas (I, II, III) help develop the message; and the subpoints (A, B, C) do the same for their respective main ideas. The arrows show the logic embedded in a well-structured talk. Everything points back to and proves the message.

2. Bring Your Arguments Together in a Recognizable Pattern

The difference between a grocery list of points and a persuasive argument is how the parts relate to the whole. When you create an effective argument, you build a case where each of the supporting points ties back to the message. The final section of this chapter presents the five basic patterns of organization. When you use any one of them, your argument builds—and, most importantly, all the points relate back to the message.

Here's one example of how the parts fit together. It's an outline that uses the Reasons model (discussed more fully in the next section of this chapter). There's a clear message, and each of the supporting points relates back to that message. Each provides a strong reason for believing in that argument.

> **Message**: I'm convinced that our company is well positioned for growth.
>
> I. We're in the right markets.
>
> II. We've developed strong customer relationships.
>
> III. We have an able, dynamic management team.

3. Think of Your Structure as Scalable

It's vital to have a sense of structure that allows you to expand and contract the length of your remarks depending on the opportunity. Carl Condon, Vice President of Technology Development for Bell Canada, asked us to work with his senior people so they could "scale" their structure to their audience. If the executives they were pitching to said "I only have three minutes" or "give me the highlights" they could do so. Knowing what your key proof points are enables you to deliver the body of your talk whether you have 30 minutes or 30 seconds. When your time shrinks, simply turn your presentation into a leadership conversation, and deliver the message and key proof points by themselves, without the supporting information.

4. Write Down Your Structure—or in Impromptu Speaking, Work It Out Mentally

Whether you are delivering a formal speech or speaking from notes, map out your structure. For formal occasions, you should no more think of "winging" your structure than you should try thinking up your message on the spot. Expectations are high and lack of preparation is a recipe for disaster.

Of course, there are times when you will be speaking off-the-cuff, or making a point in that brief elevator ride. In those instances, take a tip from Winston Churchill. Sir Winston once took a cab to a meeting, and paused before getting out. The driver announced, "You 'ave arrived, governor. You're 'ere." "I know, I know," replied Churchill. "I'm just preparing my impromptu remarks."[3]

5. Lead into the Body with a Structural Statement

Audiences want to listen, but they need your help! To guide them through your structure, give them a roadmap at the outset. The last sentence of your Introduction should be a structural statement that lets your listeners know what route you (and they) will be taking through the Body of your script. If you plan to use Reasons (see example above), you might say, "Let me give you three reasons why I say that." Or in the case of Ways, you might say, "There are four ways we're addressing that need." If you are speaking off-the-cuff, you may not know how many points you'll be making, so simply say, "We are doing several things to achieve this goal."

Five Patterns of Organization

The final step in achieving a coherent, well-organized structure is to make use of the patterns of organization discussed in this section.

Over the years The Humphrey Group has coached thousands of individuals and helped them with their formal and informal scripts. From this work, we've found that five patterns of organization provide the structure for virtually every communication. The first two, Reasons and Ways, are the most common—and were the ones introduced above. But you should know all five approaches so you can always choose the right way of structuring your argument.

Here are the five, with examples of each.

Reasons

This pattern supports your message by providing the reasons you believe (and others can believe) in your argument. Think of this as the model to use when you want to explain WHY your message is true.

> **Message:** I believe we have a very strong future.
>
> **Structural Statement:** There are three reasons I say that.
>
> I. Markets for our products are improving.
>
> II. We have a leadership position in our industry.
>
> III. We will reap returns from capital investments made in the past five years.

Ways

This pattern advances the message by showing the ways something can be accomplished. Think of this as the model to use when you want to explain HOW your message can be implemented. The following example is taken from a graduation speech by Jeff Immelt, CEO of GE.[4]

Message: I learned right here at Dartmouth how to build a life where I could do my best without ever losing a sense of the person I want to be.

Structural Statement: There are five ways to do this.

I. First, commit to learn everyday.

II. Second, work hard with passion and courage.

III. Third, be a giver.

IV. Fourth, have confidence.

V. Finally, be an optimist.

Situation and Response

This pattern makes a case for change. The first part of this pattern describes a challenge or an opportunity. The second part defines the action or solution being undertaken in response to that challenge. The following script comes from a presentation by a human resources executive.

Message: The level of dissatisfaction expressed in the last employee survey points to the need to take bold new steps.

Structural Statement: I'll first look at our challenge as revealed in our employee feedback, and then I'll discuss the steps we'll take to address these concerns.

I. [Situation/challenge] Over 60 percent of employees in our fabrication plant and call center expressed dissatisfaction with their working conditions.

II. [Response] After studying best practices in the industry, we propose a series of changes for employees in both locations.

Present Results and Future Prospects

This pattern is what we think of as an "update." It is divided into two parts. The first brings the audience up to date on the progress of a project or other undertaking. The second part shows what you expect to take place going forward. This structure is often used in annual meeting speeches, quarterly updates, performance reviews, or project reports. It shows "where we've been" and "where we expect to be." It forms the basis of the outline below.

> **Message:** If we are to build on the success we've had this past year, we must intensify our efforts to become the global leader in agricultural production.
>
> **Structural Statement:** I will talk first about how we did, and then about what we must do.
>
> I. Thanks to you, our company had splendid results last year.
>
> II. We must build upon the momentum we've gained and make the next year a period of even more impressive growth.

This is also an excellent model to follow when current results are *not* very good. Admit the difficulties of the past, but then emphasize your confidence in the future.

Chronological

This pattern emphasizes the unfolding of a process, and is particularly useful when describing how something (a company, a strategy, a country) has changed over time. The following outline is based on President Clinton's first inaugural address.

Message: We now must demonstrate the vision and courage to reinvent America, the world's longest-lived democracy.

Structural Statement: Our history is one of greatness.

I. [Past] Our founders boldly declared our independence to the world, knowing full well that America, to endure, would have to change.

II. [Present] Although our economy remains the world's strongest, we're weakened by business failures, stagnant wages, increasing inequality, and deep divisions among our own people.

III. [Future] We pledge an end to the era of deadlock and drift, and the renewal of America.[5]

These five patterns will help you organize your arguments. How do you know which one to choose? Consider your message, your supporting material, and your audience. Based on that assessment, choose the pattern that will best prove your message. For brief and informal scripts, all you'll need will be one set of points. But for longer and more formal scripts, you'll want subdivisions, too.

When you have multiple levels of organization in a script, you may use different patterns for your overall structure and for your subpoints. Every time you subdivide a point you are free to select any of the five patterns.

A final note about structure: the audience needs to hear it. *You* can see it on the page, but *they* can't. So constantly let them know where you are in your script. Flag the message as we have discussed. Give your listeners guidance on your structure.

When you use Reasons, say up front the number of reasons you will be using and preface each reason with an introductory phrase: "The first reason I believe that . . . The second reason . . ." and so forth. The same holds for Ways: "The first way . . . The second way . . ." And, if you're using Situation/Response you might say, "Here's a situation we face . . ." and "Here's our response." For Present Results/Future Prospects and Chronological, use transitions that have temporal meaning. And if you really want your structure to work for your audience, incorporate the language of your message into your structural points as much as you can. For example, don't just say, "First" or "My first reason," but say "My first reason for believing we will eradicate malaria is . . ." That way your key message is clearly reflected in your supporting points.

The Body of your script should be an act of persuasion. Its role is to drive home your message. Whether you are speaking formally or off-the-cuff, the Body is your opportunity to set forth your best arguments. Master these techniques for structuring your script, and you're well on your way to speaking like a strong leader. Your intelligence will resonate with every argument you make. And nothing is more critical to your leadership than such clear thinking. After all, ideas are the new capital of today's organizations and this set of techniques will give you abundant currency.

CHAPTER 13

CLOSE WITH A CALL TO ACTION

On January 20, 1961, John F. Kennedy concluded his inaugural address with the following words:

> In your hands, my fellow citizens, more than mine, will rest the final success or failure of our course. . . . The energy, the faith, the devotion which we bring to this endeavor will light our country and all who serve it—and the glow from that fire can truly light the world. And so, my fellow Americans, ask not what your country can do for you—ask what you can do for your country.[1]

More than 50 years later we still remember that stirring call to action, expressed in simple, clear language. Not every call to action needs to be so poetic or so visionary, but whether you're giving a speech, making a presentation, or sending an e-mail, you need to finish with a call to action.

What Is a Call to Action?

The call to action is the final element in The Leader's Script. It immediately follows the restated message, and it tells your audience what is needed to turn your message into reality. Your goal as a leader is to energize your audience. The call to action focuses that energy toward clear and specific actions that people can undertake, so that your vision (as expressed in your message) can become a reality.

Closing with a request may sound obvious, but many speakers fail to ask anything of their audience. A participant in one of our courses recalled a speaker who had initially impressed her. "He was so vibrant and passionate," she said, "and I thought, 'Wow! I want to be able to speak like that!'" Our instructor asked her, "What did you do when he had finished speaking?" The participant thought for a moment, and then said, "Well, it was the end of the day, so I went home." That individual might have been a great speaker, but he wasn't a great *leader*.

Who Should Act?

You'll want to direct your call to action to those who can best follow up on your message. The most frequent call to action is directed to your audience, but your guidance can also be self-directed (you act for your audience), or it can be combined (you and your audience both act).

An audience-directed call to action asks your listeners to act upon what you have said. Such requests range from a politician's demand, "Vote for me!" to a lawyer's insistence that the jury acquit her client. In a business setting, your call to action might be asking your audience to embrace your vision, approve a budget, review a proposal, undertake research, or accept a job position. Even something as simple as sending out the minutes of a meeting should have a call to action: "Please review the attached minutes and let me know of any amendments by Friday."

A self-directed call to action explains what *you* will do to act upon your message. This is the approach to use when it would be presumptuous to ask the audience to act. For example, a CEO speaking to shareholders cannot say, "Buy our stock." But the CEO can tell his shareholders: "My management team and I will act to continue transforming this company into an industry leader." Similarly, a junior creative director applying for a job cannot say: "Hire me." But she might conclude by saying: "I am excited about this position, and if given the opportunity I will put in long hours and give you my best work." A call to action may also be self-directed if the speaker is the focus of the script. Such was Nelson Mandela's stirring call to action, when he was on trial and about to be sentenced to life in prison: "I have cherished the ideal of a democratic and free society in which all persons live together in harmony and with equal opportunities. It is an ideal which I hope to live for and to achieve. But if needs be, it is an ideal for which I am prepared to die."[2]

A combined call to action rallies various individuals or groups. You might close a sales call with, "I would be pleased to work with you to achieve the goals we have discussed," or even more simply: "Let's make it happen!" You can offer to do one thing and ask the audience to do another. One executive closed his report to the board with the following call to action: "I'll report back to you on long-term prospects, but we need to move on the interim financing to keep this oil rig operating during the next four weeks."

You can also target multiple groups with your combined call to action. Particularly for formal remarks, there may be several audiences. Kennedy's famous call to action cited earlier in this chapter called not only upon individual Americans ("ask not what your country can do for you—ask what you can do for your country") but also upon "my fellow citizens of the world" to "ask not what America will do for you, but what together we can do for the freedom of man." Finally, it called upon God, "asking his blessing and his help."

Qualities of a Call to Action

A call to action is the rallying cry of your remarks. But to be effective, you must make it clear, practical, and inspiring.

Make It Clear

Your request should be unmistakable. If you want your audience to approve a budget, a simple, "I'd like your support" could be ambiguous. What kind of support are you looking for? If you want approval for the budget, say, "This budget will ensure that we and our stakeholders are able to reach our goals this coming year—and so I ask you to approve it." If you are a financial adviser speaking to potential customers, you might end with a call to action that says, "I would be delighted to hear from those of you who have found tonight's presentation stimulating."

Meetings, too, should end with a clear call to action. Sum up what was concluded and outline next steps. Unfortunately, too many leaders simply bring the meeting to an end with "Let's have another meeting." Participants then rush away to their next meeting, without any clear resolve to do anything. If you are leading a meeting, make sure it concludes with a clear call to action. For example: "Let me sum up next steps: bringing our currency funds in-house and hiring a team to manage them." Or "Let's form a subcommittee to create a more diverse organization through hiring policies."

Informal communications like phone calls, elevator chats, and e-mails should also end with a clear call to action. Too often e-mails or phone calls close with a weak request ("Please let me know if you have any questions") or ("Do not hesitate to contact me for further information"). Instead, end your e-mail by stating: "I look forward to your commitment to this project." In an elevator chat a clear call to action might be: "Let's get together to discuss that issue. I'll set up a meeting."

Make It Appropriate

A good call to action is well suited to the audience and to the occasion. When India's prime minister Jawaharlal Nehru eulogized the murdered Gandhi in an address before the Constituent Assembly in New Delhi, his call to action was broad enough for the audience and spiritual enough to suit the occasion. He concluded:

> In ages to come, centuries and maybe millennia after us, people will think of this generation when this man of God trod on earth, and will think of us who, however small, could also follow his path and tread the holy ground where his feet had been. Let us be worthy of him.[3]

A CEO turning around his company might end with the following appropriate call to action directed to his senior team:

We are good and getting better. Your success, and your commitment to success, are the reason I'm here. I want to thank all of you for what you have done so far, and to encourage you to continue to work to achieve our potential, yours and mine.

An appropriate call to action may also at times be a stern warning, as in the following e-mail from a senior executive to a supplier:

> I ask you to accept that we need an exclusive relationship with you—that we cannot give you our business if you are also working with one of our competitors. Unless the situation changes, we regrettably will have no choice but to sever ties.

Make It Motivational

The best leaders end inspirationally, and so should you. Certainly it's appropriate to tell the board of directors: "Other members of the team and I look forward to your full approval of the budget," but in other cases, when you are dealing with employees or other stakeholders, you'll want to put more emotion into your request. Take a leaf from the great speeches. Almost all of them appeal to the audience's hearts as well as their heads. Abraham Lincoln concluded the Gettysburg Address by saying:

> We here highly resolve that these dead shall not have died in vain— that this nation, under God, shall have a new birth of freedom—and that government of the people, by the people, for the people, shall not perish from the earth.[4]

Prince Harry of Wales paid tribute to his mother, Diana, Princess of Wales, on the 10th anniversary of her death. His call to action was moving:

> We both [Harry and William] think of her every day. We speak about her and laugh together at all the memories. But put simply, she made us, and so many other people, happy. May this be the way that she is remembered.[5]

You don't have to be Lincoln or Prince Harry to put emotion into your call to action. Here's Steve Dyer, the CFO of Agrium, speaking to his colleagues in senior management:

> Agrium is transforming itself into a truly global company. As we move forward, my team will work with you and your teams so that together we can use our strong and diverse employee base to support the growth of Agrium and transform this amazing company into a still stronger global leader.[6]

The call to action is the culmination of The Leader's Script. And here is my call to action for this chapter! The next time you prepare a presentation, make a phone call, or write an e-mail, ask yourself, "What do I want to happen?" Write that down first, and keep it in mind when you plan the rest of your remarks. Follow the guidelines in this chapter and your speeches, presentations, e-mails, and meeting comments will inspire people to follow your direction. Each act of speaking will become an act of leadership.

STEP 3

USE THE LANGUAGE OF LEADERSHIP

- ◆ Speak with Clarity
- ◆ Take the "Jar" out of Jargon
- ◆ Be Conversational
- ◆ Be Personal
- ◆ Be Eloquent
- ◆ Don't Be . . . Um . . . Tentative
- ◆ Take the Numb out of Numbers
- ◆ Jokes Are Not for Leaders

CHAPTER 14

SPEAK WITH CLARITY

In *Alice's Adventures in Wonderland*, Alice has a discussion with the March Hare and the Mad Hatter.

> "Say what you mean," the March Hare went on.
>
> "I do," Alice hastily replied; "at least—at least I mean what I say—that's the same thing, you know."
>
> "Not the same thing a bit!" said the Hatter.[1]

Like Alice, speakers often mean what they say. They've said *something*, and believe they're communicating. But too often that message is hidden. They haven't said what they mean. Their listeners remain puzzled and unconvinced—and that's a grave problem. Even the best script won't persuade listeners without clear, forceful language: the language of leadership.

This section of the book discusses how to take your script and bring it to life with language that is clear, conversational, personal, and eloquent. These chapters also show you how to avoid jargon, numbers that numb, tentativeness, and inappropriate humor. This exploration of language begins with clarity, because that quality is so important. When words are imprecise or poorly chosen, leaders lose their audience and their credibility. This chapter will discuss why speakers so often lack clarity, and the solutions to this problem.

A Lack of Clarity

Lack of clarity is the most common language problem we in The Humphrey Group encounter. It affects the broadest range of communications—including speeches, presentations, and off-the-cuff remarks.

The roots of this problem can be deep. Many leaders begin their careers with technical training, but without extensive experience in expressing themselves orally or in written form. It's possible to receive a university degree, even an advanced one, and write few essays—and present few oral reports. Organizations that rely on PowerPoint encourage information overload rather than brief, clearly constructed talks.

Much time is wasted and messages lost because leaders do not express themselves with clarity. Take the following passage from a corporate speech:

> Our selling strategy must support the combining of services. It should allow us to integrate information and apply different pricing schemes to answer customer needs. Then by developing and offering tools to better manage all our activities, we will increase customer satisfaction and loyalty.

There's meaning lurking in this passage, but it's well hidden by thick verbiage. When I asked the executive who wrote this talk about the meaning of those words, he looked at the passage as if thinking about it for the first time. Then he came up with a much better version.

> Our company should bundle its services, and not just sell them separately. If we do that, we can offer our customers better prices and greater convenience. We'll increase customer satisfaction and loyalty.

That's much clearer. And that clarity is one of the keys to persuading your listeners.

Always Be Clear

How can you make sure your audience understands you? Follow these guidelines.

1. Think Before You Speak

Too often people talk before they have formed their ideas fully. This is true particularly in impromptu interactions, such as phone calls, meetings, elevator conversations, and Q&As, as well as in the narration of PowerPoint slides. The result is often verbiage that is disorganized and difficult for the audience to follow. Chapter 7 talks about the importance of commitment. Clarity comes from putting in those hours preparing a speech, or simply pausing to collect your thoughts before answering a challenging question or speaking up at a meeting.

2. Always Be "On Message"

The best speakers are always on message, and they back up their contentions with strong supporting arguments. The guidelines for message and structure (presented in chapters 11 and 12) are important not only for the overall shape of your talk, but also for your paragraphs and sentences. Clarity involves more than simply choosing the right words. The clearest speakers stay on message and present evidence in a well-structured manner. Compare the following answers from an executive. In the first instance she has no overarching point of view. In the second she has a message that infuses her language with clarity.

> **Question from a manager:** Since the results from my group are excellent, why has our budget been cut?
>
> **Answer from a divisional executive:** [Lacking a message] We could give every department a proportional cut. If everybody takes their share, which ends up being about a 10 percent cut, we're going to find that divisions like the ones that are causing the pressures, don't have the opportunities. But that's hard to determine. We could look at the flexibility here in terms of level of spending on a year-to-date basis—the amount of uncommitted capital. But in the end, that's not how the guys will try to figure out where to put the funds, which you know are not enough to go around.

The lack of clarity comes not so much from particular words, but from the executive's lack of a message and clear structure. Here's a response with greater clarity.

> **Answer from a divisional executive:** [With a message] To strengthen corporate profitability, the executive team has asked every department

to cut its expenditures by 10 percent. [Structure: three reasons] This corporate-wide reduction in spending will ensure we meet our target. It will also encourage every department to work smarter. Finally, it will allow not just your group but every group to achieve profitability.

3. Be Precise

Precision is crucial to achieving clarity. It means being exact about expressing your ideas. A CEO who appears in *The New York Times* with the following script is using lazy, imprecise language: "Like, we were these nobodies who started in a basement and all of these giants were trying to kill us. It was like nobody knew who we were. And now it's like we're the center of everything."[2]

In a job interview you might be asked: "Why do you want to work for this organization?" Don't answer with lazy generalizations, such as, "The job really interests me because I have been looking for an opportunity to work for an organization like yours." It's much better to be specific: "I am an executive with a social conscience. This is my dream job. This position would enable me to provide financial leadership for an organization that supports tens of thousands of people with diabetes. I can't imagine a more worthy role."

4. Be Succinct

Clarity also involves expressing your ideas succinctly. Some speakers think that extra words make their arguments clearer. In fact, additional words have just the opposite effect. If you say, "Our products are durable and hold up under any conditions and will survive pretty much whatever is thrown at them," you'll leave your listeners wondering why you've engaged in such overkill. Better simply to tell them,

"Our products are made to last." Remember, inside every fat sentence is a thin sentence dying to get out!

Long-winded explanations leave audiences puzzled. Let's say you're pitching your hedge funds to a group of investors. A rambling explanation might sound like this: "Our investment vehicles can help you by providing consistent long-term capital appreciation at an attractive risk-adjusted rate of return with less volatility than traditional equity indices and low correlation to the overall equity markets." Precision is lost in a sea of words. Better to say, "Our hedge funds offer you attractive long-term growth with less volatility than traditional equity funds." Or, a still better version: "Our hedge funds offer strong, stable returns."

Often speakers use two words when one will do, producing verbal obesity. In those cases, using pairs of words undercuts rather than enhances clarity. Business writing is filled with these pairs: "learning and development," "vision and mission," "processes and procedures." Pick the more suitable word and go with one only.

Take time to make your talks concise. The French philosopher Blaise Pascal once informed a friend: "I am sorry to have written such a long letter, but I did not have time to write a short one."[3] Your friends and listeners will thank you for taking the time to make your communications succinct.

And as you practice distilling your thinking down to its very essence, you will get better and better at it. Only a seasoned communicator like Winston Churchill could have announced the Fall of France with seven simple words: "The news from France is very bad." That's how he began his speech to the British people. According to speechwriter Ted Sorensen, Churchill's words were "very direct, honest, no confusing what he's saying, but very moving at the same time."[4]

5. *Make Your Language Appropriate for Your Audience*

Speaking with clarity requires that you have a keen sense of audience. Speakers who know their audience and assess their listeners's level of expertise can pitch their comments accordingly.

A specialist in mathematical modeling might talk to a group of seasoned portfolio managers about "tail hedging." But that same individual would be better off discussing "a strategy for hedging the company's investments against disaster scenarios" when meeting with vice presidents from other areas of the business. Lou Gehrig, in his Farewell to Baseball speech, could have told his audience, "Unfortunately, I have ALS, amyotrophic lateral sclerosis." But instead he simply said: "Fans, for the past two weeks you have been reading about a bad break I got."[5]

Knowing your audience also means watching them to see if they "get it." If they look confused or restless, your comments probably lack clarity. Slow down. Ask a question to see if they are with you, and respond to the feedback they give you. Look at their body language—if they look disengaged, they probably are. Ask for comments, feedback, and ideas.

6. *Avoid Jargon*

Jargon is the bane of business, government, and professional organizations. It consists of lazy language, inflated terminology, and phrases that get repeated so often that they lose their meaning.

Shortly after I established The Humphrey Group I was invited to sit in on a consulting firm's presentations, so I could provide feedback to them. I sat there and wondered if I was listening to English or another language—very little made sense. I asked myself if this was some kind of pseudo-language they were speaking. Yet, everyone was acting as though the presenters were clear. In another instance, one of my colleagues attended what he thought was a presentation on strategy from an oil and gas executive. The presentation began, "We need to operationalize our synergies to capture this market footprint across all geographic regions. The key drivers of this strategy are to leverage our integrated assets from downstream to upstream on a go-forward basis." As everyone nodded sagely, my colleague wondered, "Will no one say that the emperor has no clothes?" Later on the client confessed that no one really understood what this meant, but it was simply safer to nod in agreement so "everyone could go back to work."

Leaders avoid this kind of muddy thinking because they know that to inspire action they must convey clear, compelling ideas. So we have devoted the next chapter to showing you how to take the "jar" out of jargon.

Speaking like a leader means speaking with clarity, so make sure you:

- think before you speak
- stay on message
- speak with precision
- keep your remarks succinct
- make your language suit your audience
- avoid jargon

If you achieve clarity in all these ways, you will be saying what you mean, and your audience will grasp your meaning.

CHAPTER 15

TAKE THE "JAR" OUT OF JARGON

'Twas brillig, and the slithy toves
Did gyre and gimble in the wabe:
All mimsy were the borogoves,
And the mome raths outgrabe.[1]
— "Jabberwocky" from Lewis Carroll's *Through the Looking-Glass*

"Jabberwocky" is a nonsense poem. It's like the jabber—or jargon—of so many speakers. It sounds like it should have meaning, but it doesn't. And what happens when we hear such sounds? Well, we struggle to interpret them. When Alice recites the above lines to Humpty Dumpty, he does his best to figure out what they say. He says "*brillig*" means four o'clock in the afternoon—the time when you begin *broiling* things for dinner. And "*slithy*" means "lithe and slimy." Who knows? You can give Humpty credit for trying to make sense out of nonsense. In fact, that's what listeners have to do when leaders use jargon. They sit there and do their best to decode the words. But often, as in Humpty Dumpty's case, their minds can only guess at what's being said.

Many speakers say in defense of jargon: "I'm talking to people who know what I mean. Jargon is the 'shorthand' I use when I'm in the company of like-minded colleagues." The trouble with that thinking is that the speaker is essentially saying: "I don't have to be clear because others know what I'm thinking." And that's just not acceptable. Jargon puts the responsibility for clarity on the audience's shoulders—not the speaker's. And even if your audience knows the acronyms or fuzzy expressions you're using—which it often doesn't—it takes time to interpret or "unbundle" the letters and words. Meanwhile, you the speaker are moving on to your next point and leaving the audience behind.

What's the answer? Identify all forms of jargon, and edit them out of your text. Consider the following jargon-filled passage from an engineering presentation.

> In constructing and building the Sports Center, the project outcome requirement was to reengineer the structure by assessing and determining the impact of contingencies—and multiple contingencies—using mathematic models on the construction of parabolic arches that form the main shielding elements over the playing area. Meteorological and extreme ground situations were game-planned, with the necessary resolution of creating unobstructed spectator view-lines throughout the entire multi-decked structure. The goal is to have an ISO-9000 building that meets the ABA's building specifications.

This passage is a good illustration of the varieties of jargon that creep into business talks. What are the "jarring" elements?

- **Abstract words.** Speakers too often rely on abstract words like "determining the impact of contingencies" or "parabolic arches that form the main shielding elements over the playing area." Professionals— engineers, computer analysts, lawyers, accountants, and others—love their lingo. But if you use expressions like that, you won't be thinking clearly. Nor will your audience. So simplify. Say "roof" instead of "parabolic arches that form the main shielding elements over the playing area." Besides, "roof" is easier on your voice, and on your audience's ears.

- **Big word syndrome.** Many speakers use big words that they think sound more impressive. For example, "view-lines" is used above instead of the simpler "view," and "meteorological" is used instead of "weather." Never use a long word when a shorter one will do. As Mark Twain, who was paid by the word, said: "I never write 'metropolis' for seven cents, because I can get the same money for 'city.'"[2]

- **Buzzwords.** These are popular, overused terms that mean everything and nothing. For example, words like "align," "strategize," and "paradigm" can suggest different things to different people. In the above passage we see examples of buzzwords: "reengineer the structure" (what exactly does this mean?) or "multi-decked structure" (would everyone listening have the same interpretation?). To cut down the number of buzzwords, start by eliminating words that end with "ize."

- **Clichés.** These overused phrases muddle meaning and lead to lost messages. Anyone who relies on expressions like "ballpark figure," "bottom line," "viable alternative," or "operational parameters" is not speaking with clarity. Similarly, "bottom line" once had a literal meaning—net earnings, the last line on a profit-and-loss spreadsheet. But now it often means something like, "Well, what does all that amount to?" As for "viable alternative"—who would want to discuss an alternative that wasn't viable? Eliminate these tired phrases from your speech and writing—they're meaningless.

- **Noun clusters.** These groups of words are simply nouns stuck together—with the desperate hope that when combined they will say something. For example: "Project outcome requirement" in the above passage. What does it mean? Why not just say "challenge?" These clusters can grow—as one noun is piled onto another. And we see them everywhere. For example, ExxonMobil's 2010 annual report discusses an Operations Integrity Management System (OIMS).[3] What does it mean? It could be a lie detector test for all we know. The company fortunately explains that "through OIMS, ExxonMobil has achieved industry-leading safety performance and continues to improve environmental performance." Who would have guessed?

- **Acronyms.** They are jarring because the audience has to take time to figure out what they mean. The acronym IBM may not give people trouble—in fact, if you said "International Business Machines" people would have to stop and think what those words mean. But if you said "HP" for Hewlett-Packard, or "BMO" for Bank of Montreal, many people would not instantly get the reference.

The same is true for other abbreviations like M&A (mergers and acquisitions). Use them only when your audience knows them well.

Sometimes, of course, technical terms must be used—they may have no substitute. "ISO-9000" in the above passage may be the only technically correct way of expressing the point. Just make sure that if you're talking to an audience that would be unfamiliar with an acronym, you explain what it means the first time you introduce it. For example, IP can mean Internet protocol and it can mean intellectual property. Make sure your audience knows the intended meaning. The rule for acronyms is to use as few of them as possible, and if you must use them, explain them.

So, to take the "jar" out of jargon, avoid:

- abstract words
- big words
- buzzwords
- clichés
- noun clusters
- acronyms

Beware of the Jabberwocky. If you're not careful, this mythical monster will swallow you up in your own language. And then you'll undercut your capacity for leadership.

CHAPTER 16

BE CONVERSATIONAL

Mark Twain once told of a Missouri farmer who ran five times for the state legislature without winning. It seems that he practiced his campaign speeches every day while milking his cows. He referred to himself as "your humble aspirant" and to his audiences as "my enlightened constituents." He talked about "obtaining a mandate" for his "legislative mission."

Then one day a cow balked at these speeches and kicked him, causing him to bite off the end of his tongue. After that, the farmer could speak only words of one syllable. The result was that he won his next election and kept getting re-elected.[1] The farmer had learned, the hard way, an important lesson about speaking as a leader: you must be conversational. No one likes being preached at, or talked down to. Audiences are most receptive when they feel the speaker is addressing them in a warm, conversational manner.

Why People Lose Their Conversational Voice

Being conversational is so important to our authenticity, yet many people abandon their natural style when they speak. We've all seen it happen. A good friend, colleague, or executive walks to the podium, begins to talk, and we wonder: "What happened to Jack? He doesn't sound like himself!" Or in a meeting we'll hear someone who just doesn't make sense, the words are so puffed up.

Why do well-intentioned people speak like this at important events? Why do they put on language airs and use big words and long sentences? In part, the problem comes from the fact that speeches, presentations, and other forms of communication are often written documents, and people have difficulty writing out their thoughts simply, as though relating them to a friend. As well, the problem stems from an abstract image some people have of communicating as leaders. They think the language must be "elevated." Finally, there is the desire to show how much they know, how much expertise they have. Why would someone in currency trading not want to load up sentences with phrases like "forward-averaging Euro-denominated sovereign debt support"? The result is a style of communicating that is different from the way we normally speak. And that puffed-up language makes it difficult for our audience to grasp what we are saying.

Using Conversational Language

What's the answer? Think of a speech, presentation, or any other set of remarks as a good conversation. Speak to your audience the way you would speak to a close associate or family member.

People who impress us use the simplest language. Leaders know they need to reach their audiences with language that is real and genuine. Speak in a conversational way and you will come across as an authentic leader.

What exactly can you do to make your language conversational? Here are techniques for language simplification.

Use Short, Simple Sentences

The shorter the sentence, the easier it is for the audience to grasp what you are saying. Successful speakers understand this. Ronald Reagan, who was called "The Great Communicator," was a master of short, simple sentences. Note how natural the following passage sounds. Reagan is addressing the nation after the destruction of the space shuttle *Challenger*.

> We've grown used to wonders in this century. It's hard to dazzle us. But for twenty-five years the United States space program has been doing just that. We've grown used to the idea of space, and perhaps we forget that we've only just begun. We're still pioneers. They, the members of the Challenger crew, were pioneers.
>
> And I want to say something to the schoolchildren of America who were watching the live coverage of the shuttle's take off. I know it is hard to understand, but sometimes painful things like this happen. It's all part of the process of exploration and discovery.[2]

This passage has virtually no complex sentences—no "which's" and "although's." The sentences in this passage average 11 words. That's good conversational prose.

Eric Schmidt, former Google CEO, used simple sentences when he announced that he would step down and the youthful Larry Page, one of the firm's founders, would take over as CEO. He said: "I believe Larry is ready. It's time for him to have a shot at running this." And he tweeted: "Day-to-day adult supervision no longer needed!"[3]

The shortest sentences we use in conversation are not technically sentences at all—they're sentence fragments that can be as short as one word: Why? How? Really? Absolutely! These short expressions help you create a conversational tone. Whether you are talking on the phone, writing e-mail, tweeting, speaking at a meeting, or presenting with PowerPoint, cut your sentences to the bone. A good example is the following "before" and "after" of a PowerPoint slide. In the "before," the bullets are too long and clumsy.

Before

We Commit to the Achievement & Maintenance of Top-Tier Safety Performance Standards.

- Employee safety will be prioritized as important in all areas in which we do business.
- Continue to operationalize and enhance safety programs.
- Build on quality management systems for ensuring contractor safety.
- Continue to improve and monitor pipeline & facilities safety.

And here's a more conversational approach, which is easier to grasp, warmer, and helps the presenter sound more natural.

After

Safety is our #1 priority. Our commitments:

- Minimize workplace accidents.
- Strengthen safety programs.
- Improve contractor standards.
- Monitor pipelines and facilities 24/7.

Whenever you are speaking (or preparing your script), think "short sentences." Your audience will appreciate it and will understand you better.

Use Short, Familiar Words

Your words, too, should be short and plain. Your audience will connect with your ideas if you clothe them in plain words. John F. Kennedy favored short, conversational words. In his famous inaugural speech, about 70 percent of the words are one-syllable.[4] This devotion to short words was deliberate. Kennedy had asked his speechwriter, Theodore Sorensen, to study the secret of Lincoln's Gettysburg Address, and Sorensen concluded that "Lincoln never used a two- or three-syllable word where a one-syllable word would do."[5] Together they created sentences like the following: "Ask - not - what - your - country - can - do - for - you - ask - what - you - can -do - for - your - country." All are single syllable words except "country."

Whether you are writing an e-mail, offering an idea in a meeting, or delivering a presentation, use short words. As Winston Churchill said: "Broadly speaking, short words are best, and the old words, when short, are best of all."[6] Look at the following example:

> **Before:** "Currently we are putting pressure on our supplier in order to expedite the chip delivery schedule. However, because the new specifications are different than the ones we previously provided, they have to add an extra process and that will take considerable time."

Now look at the next example, where longer words and phrases like "currently" and "in order to" and "however" are replaced with shorter words like "now" and "to" and "but."

> **After:** "We're now pressing our supplier to speed up chip delivery. But the new specs require a new process. That will take some time."

Your audience will appreciate it when you use everyday language. One executive we worked with mastered this principle of using short, familiar words. He spoke at a major technology conference, and the media later that day commended him for his simplicity of language: "The Senior Vice President opened COMDEX today talking about his company's mission: 'We want to bring people closer together, simplify their lives, better serve them.' A simple talk as opposed to that delivered at the end of the day by an executive who does not have the habit of simplifying."[7]

Include Informal Expressions

To convey a conversational tone, use the same informal expressions that you would use in everyday conversations. Use transitional words like "and," "now," "well," "but," "yet," and "so" to begin sentences.

Here's a good conversational example: "*Now*, don't expect this change to happen overnight. *But* it will happen." Use contractions by combining two words in one, as in "it's," "we're," "we've," and "we'll." Just remember not to become so informal that you lose your leader's tone. For example, avoid such casual words as "nope," "yep," "whatever," "hey," and "you guys."

These fundamentals of conversation—short sentences, familiar words, and informal expressions—will help you reach your audience and sound like an authentic leader. And if someone gives you a script that is not conversational, edit ruthlessly. Abraham Lincoln had his secretary of state, William Seward, prepare the first draft of his inaugural address. Then Lincoln turned this draft into plain talk. He saw the line: "We are not, we must not be, aliens or enemies, but fellow-countrymen and brethren." He changed this lengthy sentence to: "We are not enemies, but friends. We must not be enemies."[8]

Learn from the greats—famous and familiar leaders—and you'll find that you'll acquire a more authentic speaking voice. You'll begin to sound like yourself.

CHAPTER 17

BE PERSONAL

The best leaders establish warm ties with their audience. They get personal. The better the relationship you create, whether you're speaking to a thousand people or to one person, the more likely you are to persuade. One of the keys to strengthening those ties is using "I," "you," and "we." Let's look at how you can do so.

Put Yourself into Your Remarks Using "I"

Using "I" shows your personal convictions. For example, you might say "I want to talk to you about," "I believe," or "I'm convinced." Bill Clinton frequently laced his speeches and off-the-cuff remarks with "I believe." For example, in his address to Congress on health care reform, he tells his audience:

I believe as strongly as I can say that we can reform the costliest and most wasteful system on the face of the Earth without enacting new broad-based taxes. I believe it because of the conversations I have had with thousands of health care professionals around the country, with people who are outside this city but are inside experts on the way this system works and wastes money.[1]

We feel the power of Clinton's thinking because he states it as a personal conviction.

Speakers who want to put "I" into their speeches can also tell stories that take the audience into their world and show their leadership. The following story was delivered to shareholders by IBM chairman and CEO Lou Gerstner, a year after he joined IBM.

It wasn't too long after I took this job a year ago that I was struck by two things: The first was how deeply everyone felt about getting IBM back on its feet—not just here in North America, but around the world . . . Everywhere I went, it wasn't just employees and customers and shareholders who felt strongly about fixing IBM. Business people, politicians—even some of our competitors—said IBM was a worldwide institution that had to be saved. The second thing that struck me soon after I arrived here was how much free advice I was getting . . . Some said break it up, like the Baby Bells. Revive the mainframe. Get out of mainframes. Concentrate on the consumer market. Become a services company. Remain a hardware company. The best advice I got was from someone whose opinion I valued a lot—a Nobel Laureate. He poked his finger in my chest and said, "IBM is an international treasure. Don't screw it up, Lou."[2]

This personal account of Gerstner's early days at IBM portrays him as a leader who listens, who avoids snap decisions, and who is driven to find strategic solutions.

Stories can connect you to the audience by revealing the challenges you've faced and overcome. A poignant example of the "warts and all" approach to personal stories is the following story told by Jeffrey Immelt, CEO of GE, in a speech to Dartmouth University graduates.

> Ten years ago I was going through a tough patch and my boss, Jack Welch, said to me, "You know, Jeff, I love you, but if you don't improve I'm going to fire you." That really got my attention . . . I realized that I was responsible for my own success and that every day offers a new beginning. I was confident in my ability to improve.[3]

The fact that he was standing in front of his audience as CEO of global giant GE was evidence that he had faced that challenge and surmounted it.

Stories using "I" don't have to be long. You can interject into your scripts brief personal anecdotes about "what keeps me awake at night" or "why I love this company." The point is to bring yourself into your scripts and use stories to convey your leadership.

But beware of inappropriate uses of the first person:

- Avoid overuse of "I." I once interviewed someone for a position, and in his follow-up letter he began all eight paragraphs with "I." This was a signal to me.
- Don't use "I" in a boastful or imperious way. Avoid saying "I have some important shareholders to meet with, so I can only spend

a few minutes with you," or "I told you to do that . . . why didn't you . . .?"

- Avoid using "I" in a self-deprecating way ("I know I am not the speaker you hoped to have today, but . . .").

Any of these negatives will undermine your leadership and people's confidence in you. "I" can be a powerful means of letting your colleagues, customers, and staff get to know you as a leader. Just make sure that you use it with that goal in mind.

Use "You" to Engage Your Audience

Speakers need to refer to their audience as directly as possible. I once sat through a speech by a CEO to 300 of his employees and he kept referring to the firm's employees as "they"—as though they were outside the room.

Whether you're speaking to overworked employees, long-suffering shareholders, understanding customers, or young people, you can encourage your audience to "keep the faith" by using personal language. In fact, in your next speech or presentation, try lacing "you" into the talk. You can speak directly to your audience by saying: "I know all of you in this room have a strong belief in what we do, and share the goals of this great company." Or a team leader can remark: "I want to say to all of you on my team, I am very proud of you. I am very proud of what you have done."

The power of "you" is also found in informal speaking. The more you refer to your audience, the more they will listen to you. A sales manager in the "before" script below is focused on his firm; but in the "after" version he speaks more directly to the client, and is much more likely to make the sale and build the relationship.

> **Before:** We have an excellent product for you, our MPLS circuitry. That stands for Multiprotocol Label Switching. It resides on the server and will add four degrees of functionality, including backward and forward capability to your legacy system.
>
> **After:** I'm glad you shared your needs and budget with me. You have invested a lot in your videoconferencing system, and you deserve to have it work the way you want it to. We can deliver a solution, based on MPLS circuitry, that will give you the capacity and speed you need.

Here's another example, drawn from a success story. An executive we coached was making his pitch for a multimillion-dollar contract. There were four other bidders. The last question each supplier was asked was this: "In 10 words or less, why should we choose your firm?" The other suppliers stumbled in their responses. But our client was ready. He said: "We're the sole provider of peace of mind for you." Considering the complexity of the deal, that was the reassurance the company needed. They chose him.

In all forms of communication, keep a "you" focus and reach out to your audience. This could mean telling someone in an e-mail, "I got your note, thank you," rather than not replying. Or it could mean saying in a one-on-one meeting, "I appreciate your completing this report on schedule," before you challenge their thinking. Or beginning your answer to a question with, "I hear you," or "I know exactly where you're coming from," or "If I were in your position, I'd probably feel the same way."

Using "you" might also mean reinforcing the positive things your team has done. For example, "All of you on this team who have contributed to this project deserve credit for the magnificent job you have done. You have created a product that will take our industry to new heights. You are making us an industry leader."

Always remember to keep "you" references positive. As a leader you are building relationships with others. Avoid expressions like "You are wrong," "You can't be serious!" or "I disagree with you." "You" is a powerful tool. Use it in a way that engages and inspires.

Use "We" to Create a Connection with Your Audience

Used effectively, "we" brings the speaker together with the audience.

Just before taking off on space shuttle *Endeavour*'s last mission, commander Mark Kelly observed:

> As Americans, we endeavor to build a better life than the generation before and we endeavor to be a united nation. In these efforts we are often tested. It is in the DNA of our great country to reach for the stars and explore. We must not stop.[4]

This was a rallying cry to Americans to continue "reaching for the stars" and to continue the space program, which was concluding with this flight.

You can build rapport and a common bond when you use "we." For example, when you are talking to an employee you can incorporate "we" into the discussion by saying, "We both want this to work," or "We are both committed to seeing this project through."

When you use "we," always make sure you do so with great clarity. Otherwise it might become the "royal we," which sounds—unless you're the Queen—rather haughty. So introduce that pronoun by saying, "we in senior management," or "we on the leadership team," or "we—you and I together."

Be personal. It will help win you friends and allow you to influence people. And as this chapter suggests, one of the best ways of building those ties is through the effective use of "I," "you," and "we."

CHAPTER 18

BE ELOQUENT

Thanks to you [the glass ceiling's] got about 18 million cracks in it and the light is shining through like never before.[1]
　—Hillary Clinton

[The iPod] didn't just change the way we all listen to music, it changed the entire music industry.[2]
　—Steve Jobs

The most effective leaders make full use of the power of the English language. They lift up their audience with eloquence. Such language is more memorable. It influences listeners, commands their attention, and encourages them to act. John F. Kennedy's unforgettable line, "And so, my fellow Americans, ask not what your country can do for you—ask what you can do for your country,"[3] uses the Greek rhetorical figure *antimetabole*, inverting the order of repeated words.[4]

Imagine if Kennedy had instead spoken these words: "Rather than developing an 'entitlement mentality' and relying on government services, all of us should try to make our country a better place to live in." Few would have remembered his message.

While rhetoric, which is a key to eloquence, may sound forbidding, it's not. It can be as simple as a metaphor (Hillary Clinton's comment above) or the use of repetition (Steve Jobs's remark). The Roman orator Quintilian underscored the importance of rhetoric. He observed that figures of speech "add force to our thoughts and confer a grace upon them."[5] This chapter explores how rhetoric can make your scripts more powerful and help you persuade your listeners. It looks at five figures of speech, beginning with metaphor.

Metaphor

A metaphor is a figure of speech that works by linking two dissimilar things. Aristotle tells us that metaphor conveys "liveliness . . . by the further power of surprising the hearer, because the hearer expected something different."[6] One of the most famous uses of metaphor in oratory is Winston Churchill's "Iron Curtain" speech, which compares the division between the capitalist and the communist worlds to a hard, impenetrable curtain.

Ursula Burns, CEO of Xerox Corporation, used the metaphor of a family to highlight her view of the company, and how it had to change. The problem, she said, is that Xerox has developed a culture of "terminal niceness . . . we are really, really, really nice." She said employees should act more like a real family. "When we're in the family, you don't have to be as nice as when you're outside of the family . . . I want us to stay civil and kind, but we have to be frank—and the reason we can be frank is because we are all in the same family."[7]

Such metaphors create vivid imagery. Mike McCurry, President Bill Clinton's press secretary, avoided alienating reporters with "No comment," when he used the following vivid metaphor: "I'm double-parked in a no-comment zone!"[8]

Similarly, if you call your restructuring plan "a journey," you help your employees visualize the challenges that lie ahead. You can explain: "Last year we embarked on a journey to create a new kind of financial organization, and while the early stages were an uphill climb, we have reached a point that shows our vision has become a reality."

As intriguing as metaphors can be, not all of them work. Avoid the following:

- **Stale metaphors.** Expressions like the "information superhighway," sports metaphors like "cover all the bases" or "let's get the ball rolling," or phrases such as "this is below your radar screen" are all overused and should be avoided.

- **Mixed metaphors.** Don't begin with one metaphor, and then mix in another. For example, a technology company in announcing a new electronic network stated: "This is going to give our customers that are using our backbone the ability to put more stuff down it." He seems to have moved from backbone to throat.

- **Inappropriate metaphors.** Off-color metaphors will offend listeners. Don't say "Morale was in the toilet." If an executive said that publicly, his career would be in the toilet.

- **Sexual metaphors.** Also beware of sexual overtones, as in the expression "opening the kimono." It's just too suggestive. And watch the sexual innuendos that might be buried in terminology that you often use. For example, a financial services firm was quoted as saying: "Each of our advisers has a group of clients they deal with. Our service is very, very personalized and the results of that show through when we see the penetration of clients. Those clients are very well penetrated, well served. They don't tend to have relationships with other banks."

Use metaphors to enrich your ideas, but beware of metaphorical missteps.

Antithesis

Antithesis is the linking of opposites. Leaders use it regularly. For example, Indra Nooyi, CEO of PepsiCo, told an interviewer about the upbringing she and her sister had in Chennai, India. She said her mother "encouraged us but held us back, told us we could rule the country as long as we keep the home fires burning."[9]

Bono, the musician and philanthropist, told a Harvard University graduating class, "I'm not here to brag or take credit. I've come here to ask your help."[10]

Eduardo Saverin, co-founder of Facebook, uses antithesis twice in the following passage: "Intellectual capital, and not just monetary capital, will spawn the next great product or idea. Entrepreneurs, especially in the technology sector, will create things tomorrow that we can barely imagine today."[11] He counterposes "intellectual capital" with "monetary capital" and "create things tomorrow" with "barely imagine today." Antithesis gives this passage its rhythm and power.

Alliteration

Alliteration is the repetition of the same initial sound in nearby words. Martin Luther King, Jr. used this figure of speech frequently and with great subtlety.

In a speech given on the road from Selma to Montgomery, Alabama, he says:

The burning of our churches will not deter us. . . .

The bombing of our homes will not dissuade us . . .

The beating and killing of our clergymen and young people will not divert us . . .

The arrest and release of known murderers would not discourage us. . . .

We are on the move now.[12]

See how he repeats the "b" sound with "burning," "bombing," and "beating," and the "d" sound with "deter," "dissuade," "divert," and "discourage."

Jack Welch, former CEO of GE, used powerful language to support his thinking, and one of the most memorable alliterative expressions was "Speed, Simplicity, and Self-Confidence."[13] These words were his formula for transforming companies into more agile, productive organizations. Each word meant something, and together they expressed his transformational vision.

Alliteration is used in all the above examples to create a connection between ideas, and to show the power those ideas have when taken together as a group. Leaders of all kinds can use alliteration. For example, "Our company is looking for talent that's tough-minded and tenacious."

Repetition

Repetition is probably the most common figure of speech. Repeating key words is a powerful tool we often use in conversation to help our listeners understand what's important. Although our schoolteachers might have said "Don't repeat yourself," don't believe them. Repetition gives you power by calling attention to key words.

The president of Brazil, Dilma Rousseff, in her 2011 Oath Ceremony Speech, used repetition to great effect:

> I am here to open doors so that in the future many other women can also be President . . .
>
> I am not here to boast of my own life story . . .
>
> I am here, above all, to carry on the greatest process of affirmation that this country has experienced in recent times.
>
> I am here to consolidate the transforming work of President Luiz Inácio Lula da Silva . . .[14]

Such a powerful passage is achieved through simple repetition that any leader can use. A manager celebrating the completion of a team project might say:

> We are here to celebrate a great success story.
>
> We aren't here simply to claim credit for long hours and dedicated efforts.
>
> We are here to honor a team that has produced something wonderful.
>
> We are here to celebrate our greatest accomplishment yet.

Jeff Bezos, founder and CEO of Amazon.com, uses repetition for emphasis in the following passage: "If you look over long periods of time, look over hundreds of years, and look at the average sort of life cycle of a new technology, what you find is that it's getting compressed and compressed and compressed, so the rate of change is getting faster and faster."[15]

Rhetorical Questions

The rhetorical question is simply a question that you ask your audience, but that you don't expect an answer to. It intensifies the audience's involvement. So, every once in a while, ask a question.

Steve Jobs—a master communicator—used this technique when he introduced the iPhone at Macworld 2007. "An iPod, a phone, and an Internet communicator. An iPod, a phone—are you getting it? These are not three separate devices. This is one device, and we are calling it iPhone."[16] The question "Are you getting it?" created a connection with his audience.

Asking your audience a question keeps them on their toes and shows them that you are really talking to them.

The figures of speech described above help create a strong, persuasive style. They enliven your meaning and underscore your ideas. If you want to be eloquent and persuasive, remember not only the rules of rhetoric but also that *rhetoric rules*.

CHAPTER 19

DON'T BE . . . UM . . . TENTATIVE

Now we are present in strength on the Falkland Islands. Our purpose is to re-possess them and we shall persevere until that purpose is accomplished.[1]
  —Margaret Thatcher

I think we now have a major buildup on the Falkland Islands. Perhaps it could be a good idea, you know, to re-possess them. We may . . . um . . . carry on until we feel that purpose is for the most part accomplished.
  (A tentative version)

Margaret Thatcher and other great leaders use forceful language. If they didn't, their powerful messages would be lost in a sea of qualifiers. Weak language undercuts leadership. If Thatcher had spoken tentatively, as in the tentative version of her speech above, she would have left her listeners uninspired. Similarly, who would follow a manager who says to his people: "I thought that perhaps I could take a few minutes to walk through what we can maybe do on this project, if I could just have your attention. I will keep it short because I know you're busy."

If you want to lead and inspire others, avoid language that weakens your ideas. Watch out for the following "credibility killers" that could create tentativeness in your speeches, presentations, and conversations.

1. **Avoid prefatory qualifiers.** Starting sentences with qualifying expressions can undermine your leadership. Avoid, "It's only my opinion," "Just a thought," "I'm not sure," or "I don't have all the answers, but . . ." If you suggest to the audience that they know what you are about to say, they won't bother listening to you. So eliminate, "I'm sure you're aware," "As you well know," or "You may have heard this before." Get rid of phrases that indicate your remarks may be foolish or inaccurate. Don't say "This may be a dumb question," or "I could be wrong," or "I'm not sure this is right, but . . ." Don't provide ammunition for those who might question your remarks.

2. **Eliminate mincing modifiers.** Don't undercut your comments with modifiers that reduce the impact of what you're saying. Avoid "I'll *probably* want you to spend some extra time on this project," or "*Hopefully* we'll get to the root of this," or "I *just* want to say," or "*Maybe* my call to action should be," or "I'm *quite* satisfied." Eliminate "I'm a *bit* concerned," "It's *kind of* necessary," "I *only* thought that," or "The approach we take is *basically* two-fold." Why use modifiers that make you sound unsure or less confident

about what you are saying? Make a list of all the mincing modifiers above, and edit them out of your scripts.

3. **Watch for wiggle words.** I was first introduced to the concept of wiggle words when I was working with a major consulting firm, and the leader of a project said: "We need to give ourselves wiggle room." After that, I began to hear wiggle words everywhere. You may feel they give you breathing space, but they also cloud what you are really saying. Avoid words like "probably," "likely," "roughly," "primarily," "basically," "pretty," "sort of," "some," and "quite." For example, if you say, "We expect to achieve *some* economies of scale," what exactly does that mean? Instead, say, "We expect to achieve economies of scale." That is clearer.

4. **Avoid filler expressions.** Make sure you don't fill your pauses with words like "um," "ah," "you know," "to be honest," and "like." The use of such empty words can be a result of many things—habit, insecurity, or the desire to fill the airwaves while you are thinking. The impression these words creates is not a good one. They distract listeners from the quality of the ideas that you are delivering. They also make you sound tentative, since "umming" your way through pauses sounds like you don't know what you're saying.

5. **Delete weak verbs.** Phrases such as "I think," "I presume," "I suppose," "I'd guess," and "I'll try" lessen other people's confidence in what you are saying. Conditional verbs ("would," "could") are usually weak, too. Better to tell a client, "We can meet your needs," than say, "We could meet your needs." Past tense verbs, too, can undercut your leadership. For example, in off-the-cuff role-plays I've often heard clients say (as though addressing a meeting), "What I *wanted*

STEP 3: USE THE LANGUAGE OF LEADERSHIP

to talk about today was our priorities." It is much stronger to say, "I will talk about our priorities."

6. **Don't over-apologize.** Too often people apologize when there is no need to. Don't start a phone call with "I'm sorry to trouble you about this matter . . ." Don't apologize in meetings when you offer a comment. Managers who say "I'm sorry to interrupt," or "I'm sorry to take issue with you," weaken the impact of what they're about to say. People will not take you seriously if you're always apologizing.

7. **Don't self-correct.** Learn to speak with straightforward, declaratory sentences. Don't trip over yourself to correct your words. For example, here's an actual statement from an executive role-play: "I think there are some things—I think from my perspective there are some things—we need to learn—lessons that need to be learned . . . and some action . . . and some solutions we need to develop." Such on-the-spot revisions make the speaker sound unsure. Another type of self-correction is saying something, then qualifying it or undercutting it. "I am sure about what happened, although I don't remember the details." Or, "I believe I've summed up what the group feels . . . of course, I could be wrong." Self-correction makes us feel that we don't know what the speaker is really saying. And the speaker probably doesn't know either.

8. **Don't diminish your power at the end of sentences.** Often people end thoughts with "et cetera" or "and that kind of thing," because their minds are racing on to the next thought. Don't say "There are several things we can do to address the situation, including communicate more, and that kind of thing." Instead, complete the thought: "To address the situation we can do several things: communicate more, build consensus, and act decisively."

These language patterns should be avoided. While a single qualifier or lazy word won't be your undoing, the persistent use of weak language will shape listeners' views of you and undermine your credibility as a leader. Weak language represents death by a thousand blows, so be wary of the pitfalls discussed above—they are credibility killers. The language of leadership is strong and confident. If you use words that are firm and clear, you will project a firm and clear image. Be strong, and your listeners will feel that strength, and they will more readily accept your leadership.

CHAPTER 20

TAKE THE "NUMB" OUT OF NUMBERS

Caterpillar has posted record profit in 16 out of the last 18 quarters. 1997 sales totaled US $19 billion, with exports from the US of $6.1 billion—and with a profit of close to $1.7 billion. Our results so far this year are no less outstanding. During the first half of 1998, we achieved record sales of over $10 billion and a record profit of nearly $900 million. We expect that well within 10 years, we will be a more-than-30-billion-dollar company—and by the year 2010, more than 75% of our total sales will come from countries outside the United States—and that our US exports will reach over $10 billion.[1]

This passage is from a speech by Donald Fites, former Chairman and CEO, Caterpillar, to a *Business Week* CEO Summit. He should have taken one of his company's tractors and bulldozed these figures into the ground. Too many numbers create rough terrain for the listeners.

We expect leaders to be clear when they use numbers. Audiences often have difficulty grasping the words in a talk. Understanding numbers can be still more challenging. This chapter presents six techniques you can use to take the "numb" out of numbers.

1. Round 'Em Off

Ted Turner made headlines around the world when he gave a billion dollars to the United Nations in 1997. When he was asked why he gave $1 billion, he said "A billion's a good round number."[2] Bill Gates followed suit in 1999 by donating another round number—$100 million—to launch the Children's Vaccine Program.[3] Then Gates and Warren Buffett in 2010 launched a campaign called "The Giving Pledge."[4] They asked billionaires to give half their wealth to charity.

Great minds—and great speakers—use round numbers. Mark Zuckerberg, founder of Facebook, came up with a simple round number when he said: "Seventy percent of our users come back every day."[5] Is it exactly 70 percent? No. And it no doubt shifts from day to day. But 70 percent is a figure people can remember—and it's very impressive.

Of course, when you are communicating results, you must be accurate. But don't feel you have to take your numbers into the decimal points. The only time you wouldn't round off numbers is if the specific figure is significant. If you state, "the reliability factor of our technology is 99.99 percent," that figure can be quite different than suggesting a reliability factor of 99 percent or 100 percent.

2. Use Fewer Numbers

Edward Everett, who preceded Lincoln on the platform at Gettysburg, could have lightened up on his numbers. He said, "The whole rebel army, estimated at 90,000 infantry, upwards of 10,000 cavalry, and 4,000 or 5,000 artillery, making a total of 105,000 of all arms, was concentrated in Pennsylvania."[6] Why couldn't he have simply said, "The rebel army of over 100,000 was concentrated in Pennsylvania"?

Even when you're delivering financial or technical information, reduce your figures to a bare minimum. Then explain the few numbers you do use. Observe the transformation in the following passage.

> **Numbing numbers:** Overseas operations reported a 3.2 percent increase over fiscal 2010, with costs dropping 9.7 percent to $8,765,000, and pre-tax revenues, after special items and consolidations, rising 5.1 percent to $18,631,000.

> **Fewer numbers:** Sales from overseas operations were strong in 2010 and still better in 2011. Our pre-tax revenues of nearly $19 million are a record, and prospects look still better for next year.

Speakers frequently load up their PowerPoint slides with so many numbers that they often lose their audiences. Then why do they do it? For some, it's simpler to show a spreadsheet that already exists than to create a new one. Others load up on the numbers to "cover themselves": they feel they may be asked about some obscure statistic. The problem is that they look like information junkies, not leaders. So, a good rule of thumb is this: only show the statistics that support your argument. If you are discussing the changing demographics of your business market, and how your firm can tap into the "under 40" demographic, show only what's relevant. Don't put up graphs about cultural, financial, and educational trends.

Also present key figures as line graphs or bar charts, rather than spreadsheets. For example, if you are discussing rising profits, present a simple graph with three ascending bars. Add an arrow to emphasize the upward direction. That's it! Nothing else. When your numbers are that impressive, let them stand on their own.

3. Use Analogies

Some figures are too abstract to grasp on their own. Relate them to something else that people can grasp.

Numbing numbers: ATM or asynchronous transmission mode increases the throughput on standard telephone lines from 28.8 megabytes per second to one gigabyte.

Use of Analogy: ATM technology is a remarkable advance. To understand its impact, think of suddenly turning a two-lane country road into an eight-lane expressway—without laying any new roadways.

4. Create a Context

Show your listeners why the numbers are meaningful. When Sam Palmisano, IBM chairman and chief executive officer, spoke at the 2011 PartnerWorld Leadership Conference, he told the firm's partners:

Our company has remained a leader for 100 years by thinking, innovating and managing for the long term. This is what has differentiated IBM for a century of growth, change and historic impact . . . Just look across our industry. You will not find many technology companies that have made it for more than 25 or 30 years. Most don't make it to five or six, as you know. So our 100th year milestone is a clear differentiator from our competition.[7]

This passage sets IBM's longevity in the context of the industry, and thus shows how exceptional it is.

5. Give Statistics a Human Face

Humanize your numbers so they'll be easier for the audience to grasp. Present them in terms of people's lives.

Angelina Jolie, in a World Refugee Day address, gave a face to the numbers she put forward:

> We're here today to talk about millions of desperate families—families so cut-off from civilization that they don't even know that a day like this exists on their behalf. Millions. And numbers can illuminate but they can also obscure. So I am here today to say that refugees are not numbers. They're not even just refugees. They are mothers and daughters and fathers and sons—they are farmers, teachers, doctors, engineers, they are individuals all.[8]

6. Define Your Terms

Be sure any unit of measure you use is clear. For example, if you use "megabyte," explain it. And don't say, "that's 1 million bytes of information" if people don't know what a byte is. For some audiences, it might be best to simply say: "that's a standard unit of computer storage."

Jack Welch took time to explain the meaning of Six Sigma in a speech to shareholders. After telling his audience that GE has "embarked on the most challenging and important learning-based initiative in the history of our Company—the quest for Six Sigma quality levels," he explains: "The Six Sigma quality initiative, very briefly, means going from approximately 35,000 defects per million operations—which is average for most companies including GE—to Six Sigma, fewer than four defects per million in every process that this company engages in every day: from manufacturing a locomotive part to servicing a credit card account, to processing a mortgage application, to answering a phone."[8]

As you can see, there are many ways to take the "numb" out of numbers. But the starting point must be a concern for your audience. Numbers are not easy to absorb, so be good to your listeners. Take the numb out of your numbers, and your audience will thank you for doing so.

CHAPTER 21

JOKES ARE NOT FOR LEADERS

Great speeches, presentations, and meeting comments are not dull. They are enlivened with wit, quotations, and anecdotes. But they do not rely on canned humor or tired jokes. Jokes are not for leaders.

In too many talks, stale attempts at humor weaken rather than strengthen the ties between speaker and audience. The desire to entertain is understandable. We've all endured too many dry speeches. Hence some speakers decide to spice up their talk with a joke they heard at lunch or read in a book. But those stories regularly fall flat. And some end up embarrassing the speaker and audience.

Your goal as a leader is persuasion, not entertainment. A leader may use humor, but should not be viewed as a humorist. If your listeners see you as a jokester, they will have trouble taking your message seriously. Here are the dangers anyone introducing humor should be aware of.

1. Jokes May Insult Individuals or Groups

Such stories should not be told. Some of these jokes can be sexist or racist. These should not even be told in private company let alone in a public address. Also be careful not to offend any religious group, or even those individuals who don't believe in religion.

Is that "political correctness"? Perhaps. But I'd rather think of this suggestion as basic politeness and common sense. If you're trying to persuade your audience to accept your point of view, you must be sensitive to their feelings.

And beware, too, of taking potshots at people who aren't in the room, just for the sake of scoring with your audience. I recently attended a speech given by a male executive to 100 women. He began with a canned joke:

> A person goes into a store that sells brains—female brains and male brains. "Why," the male shopper asked, "are female brains more expensive than male brains?" "That's simple," said the clerk. "The brainpower that's in one jar of female brains is equivalent to several jars of male brains."

The women in the room laughed. But not because they thought it was a good joke. They laughed a nervous laughter, because it was a dumb joke, and it was a cheap joke that tried to score with women by putting down men. Let's just say the brainpower in that joke wouldn't have filled even the bottom of a jar.

Furthermore, don't insult yourself. It's a rare situation where a joke at your own expense is appropriate. As the Roman orator, Quintilian, wrote: "To joke upon oneself is the part only of a buffoon and is by no means allowable in an orator."[1] Some individuals reveal their insecurities with comments about how they are poor speakers or how they lack charisma. There are instances of self-deprecating humor that have a certain wit and charm. Robert Reich, the secretary of labor under Bill Clinton, was 4-foot-10, and would frequently begin his remarks saying, "I'll be short," or stand on a stool and say, "I'm the only candidate with a platform." But even Reich has been criticized for his humor by other short people who were offended.[2] Roasts, those dinners where barbs are publicly exchanged, are also dangerous terrain. My advice? Don't "roast" others, or make yourself the object of such events. If you're a public figure with a well-established reputation, such a dinner might be part of the price of your fame. But if you're in business or government, these events can turn out to be disasters. One of my clients, a CEO, was kidded—inaccurately—about her drinking habits at such an event. These statements were made by one of her executives, who drew big laughs with his remarks. But for the CEO the humor was not funny, and the offending executive had to write a public letter of apology.

By extension, don't insult groups you belong to, even in fun. Many bankers feel obliged to make banker jokes, lawyers to make lawyer jokes, and so forth. But why put your profession down? I'd also be cautious about using Scott Adams's *Dilbert* comic strip and other cartoons. Such material can be scathingly funny, but dangerous.

2. Jokes often Seem Pasted onto the Talk

How many times have you heard a speaker begin with a joke, and then when the laughter subsides say in a dreary tone: "And now for my speech." This pasted-on humor can come from books with titles such as *1001 Funniest Stories* or from talk show monologues, which seemed funny at the time. Whatever the origin of canned humor, avoid it! The best humor should fit seamlessly into the speech. It should be relevant to the business at hand.

3. Jokes are Difficult To Tell

The same story can rock an audience with laughter, or die on the page—depending on who tells it. Know your own strengths and limitations. Don't try to be funny if that is not your style. Few of us have the skills of Mark Twain, who was not only a wonderful writer, but also a witty speaker. He once told a dinner gathering in London that he was returning to the United States to run for the Presidency. He then explained that "those who have entered [the race] are too much hampered by their own principles." A successful candidate must "satisfy the whole nation, not half of it." Twain continued: "There could not be a broader platform than mine. I am in favor of anything and everything—of temperance and intemperance, morality and qualified immorality, gold standard and free silver."[3]

Stephen Hawking is also a great humorist. He speaks by touching a computer screen that translates his words through an electronic synthesizer, yet this does not prevent him from expressing humor. Talking to a White House audience about esoteric quantum concepts of probabilities and "alternative histories," he said: "There must have been a history in which even the Chicago Cubs won the World Series."[4]

So humorous stories can work in a speech, but they succeed only when used with great care—and great skill. If you can't reach those heights, the danger of falling is too great. The best principle to keep in mind is: jokes are not for leaders.

STEP 4

ACHIEVE A LEADER'S PRESENCE

- Bring Your Script to Life
- You Are the Best Visual
- The Eyes of a Leader
- Suit the Action to the Word
- Find Your Leader's Voice

CHAPTER 22

BRING YOUR SCRIPT TO LIFE

When you speak as a leader, you must energize your audience and motivate them to act upon your ideas. Your vision, script, and language—which we have discussed so far in this book—are only important insofar as they can be *brought to life for an audience.*

This section of the book, "Achieve a Leader's Presence," will show you how to inspire your listeners by making your delivery compelling and strong. These chapters emphasize the importance of energy, presenting yourself as the best visual, eye contact, body language, and voice. Once you take those steps, you will have transformed yourself from speaker to leader, and your audience from listeners to followers. The starting point is to focus on the audience, find the energy in your script, and bring it forward with an expressive delivery.

Focusing on Your Audience

Every time you speak, be aware of the tremendous source of energy gathered in front of you: your audience. It's up to you to transform that potential energy into a powerful force for change. You must make your listeners take notice of what you're saying, and inspire them to follow your lead. Audiences, in fact, want to be moved, to care, to be inspired. What audience member ever walked into a room wishing to be bored?

Yet too frequently speakers ignore that potential—and the desire of their listeners to be involved. For many speakers a concern for the audience is secondary to other preoccupations. They concentrate on the content of their talk, not its delivery. An executive preparing for an industry conference often focuses on mastering the subject matter and creating slides displaying that content rather than asking, "What's in this for my audience?" A manager getting ready for a quarterly management meeting devotes her attention to the "numbers" rather than to what those numbers can mean for the audience. *The audience doesn't figure into those preparations.* The result? Too many speakers come to see boredom as the natural state of an audience. They keep speaking the same dull way to half-asleep audiences.

The goal of speaking, instead, should be to reach out and engage the hearts and minds of your audience. This focus on the audience begins as soon as you start preparing your remarks, and it continues while you are delivering your talk. Margaret Thatcher wrote in her autobiography: "I was told that most stage actors would rather hear an audience's reaction without seeing the audience. . . . But I always insisted that from any public platform I must be able to see as well as hear how my words were being received."[1] Once you tap into the energy in the room, and move your audience with the power of your own convictions, you will feel enormous satisfaction. One of the best violinists in the world today, Nigel Kennedy, put it well when he said he wanted to "break through all this protocol stuff" and "actually make people feel what I was feeling." The result: "at the end of the performance I get this brilliant feeling: we've completed the concentrated effort and the audience reaction just washes over you like waves of warm water on a beach. It's a great feeling. I don't know how to write it down, but I promise you it's what fuels you until the next time." [2]

Find the Energy in Your Script

To energize your listeners, find the power in your script and then convey it to them. Bring your script to life for your listeners. Your job as a speaker is to *interpret* your text for your audience. If you treat every word in the script as equally important, you'll sound monotone and your audience will retain little of what you've said. Instead, bring to life the important elements of your script.

To begin with (and most significantly), emphasize the structural elements in your talk. These key components are:

- **Message.** Your message is the strongest statement in the script and should be delivered with great conviction.

- **Key arguments.** These introduce the main divisions in the Body, and should also be delivered with great emphasis.

- **Restated message.** This is the idea you want your audience to take away. Reaffirm it with conviction.

- **Call to action.** This is your rallying cry to your audience. Hit it hard.

These statements should be delivered with the greatest force and conviction. When you come to these lines, intensify your voice. Punch out these sentences. Other supporting material should be delivered with a less dynamic tone and with a faster pace than your structural elements. Think of it this way: your script consists of foreground (structural elements) and background (supporting information). Let your audience hear the difference.

Next, bring your script to life by emphasizing the "energy words." These are the words that help you make your points. They consist of verbs and key nouns, as well as powerful modifiers. If you are comparing two items, the words that form the comparison should be emphasized. ("While our earnings in North America are *modest*, our gains in Europe have *broken all records*.") If you write sentences with parallel structure, the energy words are the ones that form the series. ("Our communications program has benefited *employees*, *clients*, and *shareholders*.") The energy words are also words that emphasize your theme. If you're talking about expansionary plans for your company, the energy words would be words like "growth," "expanding markets," and "global reach."

Finally, to convey the energy in your script, pause frequently. We do that all the time in conversation. We pause mid-sentence when we want to emphasize something. We pause between items in a series. We pause before an important statement (such as our message). To indicate these stops, mark the text with a forward slash. ("Today I want to discuss this year's results / and our plans for the coming year.")

Annotate the text to indicate sentences and words you want to emphasize, and the pauses that will add force to your argument. To show you what a marked-up script looks like, see the annotations added to the historic speech below. It's an address given in

1877 by Chief Joseph, of the Nez Perce Indians, surrendering to the U.S. Army.[3] All the structural components—grabber, message, three main points, restated message, and call to action—are bolded, the energy words are underlined, and the pauses are marked with slashes. Read it out loud, by slowing down and intensifying expression for the lines that are bolded or underlined. You will hear the words on the page come to life:

Tell General Howard I know his heart. What he told me before, I have it in my heart. / **I am tired / of fighting. Our chiefs / are killed;** Looking-Glass is dead. Ta-Hool-Hool-Shute is dead. / The old men are all dead. / It is the young men who say yes or no. He who led on the young men is dead. / **It is cold, and we have no blankets;** the little children are freezing to death. / My people, some of them, have run away to the hills, and have no blankets, / no food. No one knows where they are—perhaps freezing to death. / **I want to have time to look for my children, / and see how many of them I can find.** / Maybe I shall find them among the dead. / Hear me, my chiefs! **I am tired /** my heart is sick and sad. **From where the sun now stands I will fight no more / forever.**

Use the same techniques to energize business scripts. Once again structural sentences are bolded, energy words are underlined, and pauses are marked. Guided by these annotations, read the following talk aloud.

There is a perception that investing in equities is risky business. In fact, **our funds have delivered / a strong / performance over the years.** We get these impressive results in a number of ways. **First we ensure**

that our portfolios have a good mix of investments. These equities are diversified by industry / by geography / and by the size of the companies we invest in. **Second, we carefully study the management of the firms.** We look for experience, / integrity, / openness, / and track record. / **Third, we examine the margin of safety of investments.** That's the relationship between the intrinsic value of a stock and its market price. We only invest when the market price is significantly below its intrinsic value. **So we actively manage our portfolios to ensure they deliver positive / long-term returns. We would be delighted to show you how your money can grow with us.**

By bringing your script to life, you show your audience that you believe in what you are saying—that you are connected to it.

Find the Energy within You

Once you find the energy in your script, tap into your own personal energy to bring the script to life for your audience. How do you do that? First, practice your lines—as a good actor does—before you deliver them. Read them out loud with as much energy and passion as you can find.

Our instructors often ask the leaders we rehearse to exaggerate the drama and the importance of what they are saying. We ask them to "take it over the top" in a number of ways. First, we encourage them to use larger gestures, sometimes delivering their entire short scripts or a portion of a larger script with arms fully extended. We also urge them to put far more expression into their voices, interpreting their lines in an exaggerated way, with more conviction, intensity, and color. We encourage them to project loudly, and engage the person who is in the very back of the room. Finally, our coaches help them practice strong eye contact—focusing their eyes with life and energy. Normally, when clients go through this exercise they feel out of their comfort zone. As they crank up the passion, they feel that it is "too much." But when this happens in a seminar, those listening invariably say, "It was much better, we understood the script more." And in fact, when the speaker's body is full of this newfound energy, the speaker becomes more authentic, more conversational, more sincere and credible. Often even the language changes to become more genuine. All this because inner energy is being tapped.

The Humphrey Group has many instructors with theater backgrounds because actors know how to unleash their inner energy for an audience. Leaders need to learn how to do so as well. So, the beginning of achieving a leader's presence is tapping into that force within you—that *energy of influence*. Passion engages the audience. In the end, tapping into your energy is the foundation of great delivery. Being able to open up to an audience, draw upon your "inner life," and share it with your audience is what will make you an exceptional speaker. Once you are willing to do that—once you are willing to be open, vulnerable, and real—your audience will see you as their leader. They will follow you. Such leadership not only characterizes successful corporate and organizational leaders, but it is also evident in artists, poets, conductors, entrepreneurs, athletes—anyone who can release that inner energy and passion.

CHAPTER 23

YOU ARE THE BEST VISUAL

Great speakers rarely use visual aids. Just imagine John F. Kennedy standing before the world at his inauguration with a flipchart that read: "The Torch Has Been Passed." Or Martin Luther King, Jr. showing a slide with a clip art image of a black girl and a white girl holding hands. Such props clearly have no place in these stirring speeches. In fact, they would detract from the drama of the moment.

Why? The most influential leaders understand that they are the best visual. They instinctively know that their message will come through most fully if the audience watches them—with no distractions. Looking at and listening to the speaker, audiences grasp that individual's confidence, stature, conviction, and leadership. Audiences that divide their attention between speaker and visual are only partially connected to the speaker, and only partially committed to the speaker as a leader.

Let's look at the logic behind this statement. The main goal of any business presentation, speech, or conversation should be to lead others. Of course, there are many possible secondary goals of a presentation—to entertain, to inform, or to share expertise. But if you are speaking as a leader, your chief goal should be persuading the audience to think or act differently than they otherwise would have.

The best way to persuade your listeners is to become the focal point of their attention. Presenters often use PowerPoint or other visual aids, believing that their audience can absorb more of their talk if they listen *and* look. But that's not the case. When speakers use visuals, they create competition for the audience's attention. The audience must divide its focus looking at the visual and listening to you. And because the eye is a much more powerful sensory device than the ear, the eye wins. Your visuals get star billing: what you are saying finishes a distant second in the audience's mind.

The audience needs to focus on you—they will see your commitment in your eyes, in your gestures, in the way you walk, in the way you stand, in the way you hold your head high. Your body becomes the very best visual for portraying your leadership message. We say a great leader has "presence." That is, the speaker is *present* in a way that engages everyone in the room. Many great speakers realize that being present gives them power to persuade. So they do everything they can to maximize their visibility.

President Woodrow Wilson broke with a 113-year tradition by personally reading his State of the Union address to Congress, rather than sending those remarks to be read by a clerk. His reason? He wanted to show "that the President of the United States is a person, not a mere department of the Government hailing Congress from some isolated island of jealous power, sending messages, not speaking naturally and with his own voice."[1] Later presidents followed suit, and the delivery of the State of the Union speech has become an important occasion for presidents who want to make the case for their agenda.

There are, to be sure, some instances where visual aids are important. They're needed when you're presenting a new product, as Steve Jobs did on many occasions. And in such cases you might use a prop, like the iPhone, which Jobs held lovingly in his hand, looking at it, smiling at it, and holding it up for the audience to see and admire. Such props are not distracting, because they are an extension of the speaker and support the message. And in many corporate cultures, you're expected to accompany your presentation with PowerPoint slides or other visual aids. It makes sense to do so if you have information that has to be presented in charts or graphs. But many word or even number slides undercut rather than enhance your leadership. So if you have the chance, go it alone.

Visual blight characterizes many slides and detracts from your leadership. When Lou Gerstner first became CEO of IBM, he complained: "I have never seen foils [overhead transparencies] like in this company. There must be a manual that says every foil must have four circles, two squares, two triangles, 16 arrows, and as many of them as possible should be three dimensional—with shading—and at least four colors."[2] How many business presentations have you sat through where just puzzling out the cluttered information on the screen causes you to disengage from the speaker's talk?

And if your visuals dazzle, you have another kind of problem. At a glitzy presentation given by a chief information officer of a major corporation, the speaker's state-of-the-art slides dazzled the audience. After the presentation, a member of the audience came up and asked, "Do you have a card? The card of the firm that produced the visuals? They were great!" Don't be sidelined by visuals.

Be the visual, not the aid. Hold your ground. If you want to achieve your maximum power, focus the audience's attention on yourself. Only then will you experience your full potential to reach and motivate an audience. Only then will you be a convincing leader. In the words of Humphrey Bogart, "Here's looking at you, kid."[3]

CHAPTER 24

THE EYES OF A LEADER

When the eyes say one thing and the tongue another, a practiced man relies
on the language of the first.[1]
  —Ralph Waldo Emerson

As Emerson and many other observers are aware, your eyes are a powerful means of communicating. You engage others with your eyes. They show people whether you are happy or sad, committed or bored, passionate or passive. The way you look at people is key to influencing them. The eyes are an instrument of leadership and you can use them to that end whether you are speaking from a script, from notes, or simply delivering impromptu comments.

Leading with Your Eyes

One of President Bill Clinton's great strengths as a communicator was his extraordinary eye contact. On the campaign trail, he was described by one journalist as "making eye contact so deep that recipients sometimes seem mesmerized."[2] Author Michael Ellsberg, in his book *The Power of Eye Contact*, notes that Clinton made people he looked at feel as if they "were the only people in the room."[3]

But you don't have to look to Clinton alone to understand the power of eye contact. Think of the people that most impress you with the power of their eyes. It could be a boss, a colleague, or a teacher. They truly become leaders when they look directly at you. As a parent, too, when you make strong eye contact with your children, you acquire more authority. Children are more apt to listen to you and take what you are saying seriously.

What is it about eye contact that has such an impact on people?

First, it establishes a relationship with your audience. It is part of the basic generosity of speaking, and therefore of leading. When you look at your audience, you are taking them in, centering yourself on the people who are important to you—your listeners. This is true whether you are speaking to one person or a hundred people. One of our instructors delivered a workshop to 300 people who were dispersed across a large theater-style room. As she discussed eye contact, she paused and asked the audience, "How many of you feel I have already begun to build a relationship with you?" The majority of people raised their hands, which is amazing, since she had no previous relationship with any of them and she was only a few hours into the seminar.

When you really look at people, not superficially eyeballing them or glaring at them, but really taking them in, you form a relationship. For a leader this is critical: people want to be led by someone who can look them in the eye. When you look at your audience, you are saying, "I want to be here. I want to talk to you." When someone looks you directly in the eye, it makes you feel special, and you're willing to focus on that person.

Second, eye contact enables an audience to concentrate on what you are saying. That's because over 70 percent of the body's sense receptors are in the eyes.[4] Audiences listen with their eyes. All the other senses *taken together* are unable to compete with the eyes. The relationship between good eye contact and influence is suggested by the phrase "seeing eye to eye." When we hold others with our gaze, we can more effectively get them on our side.

Is the power of eye contact universal? Some believe that strong eye contact is a Western imperative and could be off-putting in other cultures. But when The Humphrey Group introduced strong eye contact to business leaders from 13 Asian countries, they told us they *absolutely wanted* to develop the ability to look others directly in the eye as part of their leadership presence. Looking people in the eye, even in Asia, is a sign of confidence; it shows that you are comfortable with your power, which is so critical to leadership.

For all these reasons, strong eye contact is imperative for leaders. But the way you achieve it is different for each situation. Let's look at how you make eye contact with your audience when you are reading a prepared text, using a teleprompter, speaking from notes, delivering a PowerPoint presentation, or talking off-the-cuff.

Reading: The UP-DOWN-UP Technique

Even when you are reading a prepared text, you want to make strong and natural eye contact with your audience. But doing so is challenging. Some speakers don't even try. Their eyes stay glued to the page, and their tone of voice says, "I'm reading, so it's okay if I sound boring."

Other executives, showing more concern to reach their audience, bounce up and down from the page to the audience. A few—wishing to avoid these hazards of reading—memorize their speeches. But that is an onerous burden! And once you've memorized a text, all your energy is spent trying to recall the next passage.

Fortunately there's a great approach to reading verbatim yet looking as though you're simply talking to the audience. It's the UP-DOWN-UP technique. It allows you to read a speech as though you are in conversation with the audience.

To achieve this conversational eye contact, first realize that there's no need to look at the audience all the time. In normal conversation we spend only 60 to 70 percent of our time making eye contact with the people we're talking to. The rest of the time we're gazing out the window, around the room, or at the table while we marshal our thoughts. So trying to dart up from the page all the time is not natural. There's no need to do it. It will appear artificial and strained.

When should you look up from the script? Eye contact is most important at the *beginning* and *end* of each sentence. Looking at the audience at the beginning of a thought tells them that what you're about to say is worth their attention. Looking at your audience at the end of a thought encourages them to reflect upon what you have just said. We do this all the time in conversation. To emulate this conversational style, use the UP-DOWN-UP eye contact technique. With each sentence:

- Look down at the first few words in the sentence, then come UP with those words in your mind's eye and deliver them to the audience.
- As soon as you start speaking that sentence, let your eyes fall DOWN to the middle of the sentence and read it, keeping your eyes down.

- When your eyes see the end of the sentence (they will get there before your voice does) look UP with these final words in your mind's eye and deliver them to the audience.

Now one more thing: when you come up at the beginning of each sentence, don't speak immediately. If you do, it will look like you're just scooping words from the page and dishing them out to the audience. Instead, come up, pause for a second or two looking at the audience, then start the sentence. Similarly, after you have spoken the final word in the sentence, pause for a second or two, still looking at the audience. These pauses give weight to what you are saying, and strengthen your relationship with the audience.

For a short sentence—up to seven words—you won't have time to go up-down-up. So, go down, come up with the whole sentence in your mind, and after that initial pause, deliver the entire sentence looking at the audience.

For those of you who deliver speeches or scripted presentations, the UP-DOWN-UP technique will allow you to speak with power while building your ties with your audience. Our clients have had great success with this technique for reading scripts. One of them said, "I spoke to a few hundred people and they gave me warm and enthusiastic applause. A few people in the audience came up afterwards and said, 'You're great! I felt you were speaking to me personally.'"

Reading with a Teleprompter

Another way to deliver scripted texts with strong eye contact is using a teleprompter. The device consists of two transparent screens positioned to the left and right of center stage. An operator scrolls through your script, following your pace, so you can read the speech while still looking out into the audience. The teleprompter creates the illusion that you're talking to the audience, not reading. But here's the rub! You must be effective at using the teleprompter. Even a seasoned speaker like Barack Obama needs some coaching on this technique. In many of his talks, his eyes dart from one prompter to the other without ever looking at the audience (watching from TV land in between). This creates two major problems: (1) it's obvious to the audience he is reading from a prompter, and (2) he ignores his main audience—the millions of people who are watching him from their homes. If I had two hours with Barack Obama, here is what I'd tell him:

A White House Lesson

Mr. President, by all means, use the teleprompter, since you want to have your eyes out there, looking at your audience. But here's how to do it. Begin reading your first sentence from one of the prompters, and then as you are speaking that sentence, let your eyes gradually move to the center of the room and finish that thought there. Begin the next sentence looking at the other prompter, and finish speaking that sentence while focused on the audience in the center of the room. There are variations of this technique, but essentially the best teleprompter technique involves using all the space between the two prompters. In fact, Mr. President, you should look down the center of the audience half the time you are speaking, and one quarter of the time you should be focused on each side of the room. Such a delivery will look conversational and you will be truly talking to your audience, even though you're reading.

Any leader can benefit from this White House lesson. If you want great eye contact, don't dart between the teleprompter screens (and also don't stare into a camera lens when there is an audience in front of you). Use the full space—left, right, and center—to come across as a leader who is truly talking to the audience.

Speaking from Notes

Making good eye contact when speaking from notes is easier than reading from a scripted speech. But there are still techniques to be mastered.

- In your notes, keep your bullet points short so each can be seen in a glance.
- To create the best eye contact, deliver each point ALL UP. Before presenting each new idea, look down, see the point in its entirety, then come up from the page and present it. Go down for the next point, come up and deliver it looking at your audience. And so forth. This technique will enable you to deliver your material precisely, and with eye contact that is focused on the audience at all times.
- Be careful not to talk on your way up from the page. If you do so, you will not appear to be speaking authentically. You will appear to be scooping text from the page. Instead, come all the way up, look at your audience, then speak the thought.
- When you look at the audience, speak to one person at a time. Break the room down into individuals, and have "mini conversations" with each person. That way, you will really be reaching people.
- Finally, when presenting from notes, rehearse, rehearse, rehearse. You don't want to be fumbling for words or figuring out how to

expand upon your bullet points. Do all that heavy lifting before you get into the room, so your points are really just "memory joggers."

Note-form talks are a wonderful way of presenting to small gatherings, but work well only when you have prepared fully.

Speaking with PowerPoint

It's easy for PowerPoint presentations to become a snoozefest. If you've been in an organization very long, it's likely that you've sat through a few (or many) such talks. One way that you can make sure your PowerPoint talk holds the audience is by establishing good eye contact.

The first rule of delivery for such presentations is this: speak to the audience, not to the slide. Too often the audience feels like a "third party" to the conversation a speaker is having with her slides. The worst of this is when speakers actually turn their backs to the audience. Here are guidelines to keep you on track.

- Begin by glancing at the slide. Obviously, you have to know where you are in your visuals.
- Having done that, deliver your ideas just like you would in a note-form talk (see above). Grab your point from your notes—which will be reinforced by the slide—and present it to your audience with your eyes on them. Don't let your eyes drop before you have finished your point.
- If you have no notes, but are using the slide to prompt you, come out from behind the podium, glance at each new slide to catch its central point, then turn to the audience and speak that message.

If you need to consult the slide again, be sure to turn back to the audience and look at them when you are speaking to them.

Strong eye contact is particularly critical when you are delivering a PowerPoint presentation because the slide is a powerful competitor. Your leadership depends on establishing a strong relationship with the audience, rather than being regarded simply as someone narrating visuals. An audience wants to be led by someone who is looking at them.

Speaking Off-the-Cuff

Strong eye contact is important as well for impromptu speaking, including talks to small groups and remarks made in the elevator, at job interviews, or at networking events. Whatever the situation, there are fundamentals to keep in mind if you want to be perceived as a strong leader. To begin with, no matter how small the "stage" or informal the situation, good eye contact is important. Many people have poor eye contact in informal situations because they are distracted, nervous, bored, or simply unaware of the need to look at the other person. If your audience sees your gaze wandering, you'll have no chance of leading them.

When you walk into a room, the first impression you make will be shaped by your eye contact. When I meet with a new senior executive client, I often find that person testing me to see whether I can hold their gaze. The higher up they are, the longer and stronger their eye contact. To break it would be a sign of weakness. It goes back to the fact that eyes have a predatory quality and are associated with power. Diane Ackerman, in her book *A Natural History of the Senses*, writes that our eyes are hard-wired to seek out prey. "Most predators have eyes set right on the front of their heads, so they can use binocular vision to sight and track their prey . . . Prey, on the other hand, have eyes at the sides of their heads, so they can tell when something is sneaking up behind them."[5] When you meet someone at a networking event or in a job interview, shake hands and hold their gaze as long as you can. It may feel awkward, but it will convey your strength.

When speaking in a meeting, use strong eye contact to reach everyone there. Let's say you have six, seven, or even 20 people at the boardroom table. Make eye contact with one person at a time. Deliver one thought to one person, then the next thought to someone else, so that you are always making one-on-one eye contact. The power of this approach is that you create a strong connection with each person. When you build those ties, everyone else in the room will feel that personal connection. They will feel you are talking to them. This is the secret to Bill Clinton's eye contact, and it can be your strength, too.

When you're not speaking, look at the person who *is* speaking. I remember attending an annual general meeting of a pharmaceutical company. The CEO could have benefited from this advice, because while his chief financial officer was speaking, he sat there on stage, distracted first by someone coughing, then by a latecomer, then by a piece of lint on his suit. This poor eye contact sent the wrong message: that he cared more about these distractions than about what his CFO was saying. Remember: we need to have a leader's presence, even when we are not talking.

In Q&A sessions, good eye contact is also important. When responding to a question in a large room, begin by looking directly at the person who asked the question, then move on to others in the room. End your answer looking again at the questioner. This technique shows proper respect for the person who asked the question, while making everyone else feel that they are included in the dialogue.

Finally, in all the speaking situations discussed above, make sure your eyes are animated—that your eyes are truly speaking. The famous acting teacher, Constantin Stanislavski, in his book *An Actor's Handbook*, writes: "How often we actors stand on the stage and see nothing! Yet what can be more awful than an actor with vacant eyes? [Or a leader with vacant eyes!] They are such obvious evidence of the fact that the soul of the actor playing the role is dormant . . . or otherwise engaged in matters unrelated to his role."[6] If your eyes are animated, you will inspire others with your energy and excitement. They will want to follow you because they will see that you believe what you are saying.

Practice the techniques discussed in this chapter every day, in every situation from formal speeches to brief one-on-one encounters, and your eyes will become a true mirror of your leadership.

CHAPTER 25

SUIT THE ACTION
TO THE WORD

Speak the speech, I pray you, as I pronounced it to you, trippingly on the
tongue . . . Do not saw the air too much with your hand, thus, but use all
gently . . . Suit the action to the word, the word to the action.[1]
—Shakespeare, *Hamlet*

Hamlet reminds the visiting troupe, who have come to Elsinore, about the importance of body language. He emphasizes that their "actions" or gestures must reflect the words of their script. His advice is relevant for today's leaders. Strong, confident body language reinforces the messages you are delivering. This chapter looks first at why body language is so important, and then discusses how you can project your leadership by strengthening your stance, gestures, and facial expression.

The Importance of Body Language

When you address an audience, your body "speaks" for you, and it is important that your body speaks well. It must say, "I am here to lead. I have an important message to share with you." If the message your body sends conflicts with the message you are delivering, the audience will be unimpressed by your words.

Body language is extremely important for a leader's image. Just consider the following examples.

- Ronald Reagan was a master of the relaxed, conversational style. He looked the same whether he was giving a speech, being interviewed, answering a question, or just walking and talking with people. He looked directly into people's eyes, smiled warmly, and had movement in his body. His relaxed style said, "I am someone you can trust." That style earned him the affection of most Americans—including many who disagreed with his views.

- Steve Jobs had an approach that exuded controlled conviction. He worked hard to develop this laid-back but focused style. His demeanor was reflected in his casual dress, low-key pacing, and deliberate large and open arm gestures.

- Dilma Rousseff, who became the president of Brazil in 2011, projected a radiant presence when she took office. She held her head high, stood tall, and was animated. She succeeded in reaching the Brazilian people.

All these leaders have great body language, but it is different for each leader. And that's as it should be. You want your body language to be authentic to you and your vision. Still, there are essential characteristics of body language that every leader must master. You want your body language to say that you are a leader who is open and worthy of trust. It should tell listeners that you are committed to what you are saying and that you have confidence in yourself. You can achieve this leadership presence by observing the following guidelines for stance, gestures, and facial expression.

Stance of a Leader

Whether you are sitting or standing, show your stature as a leader. Be "tall" when you stand or sit. Stature is not a question of height but of attitude. Standing and sitting tall will reflect your attitude as a leader. It says, "I believe in myself," and "I am confident speaking to you."

When Standing

Leaders must be able to stand in front of others without slouching or turning away. Many people are not comfortable standing tall. They prefer a more casual stance. I once watched a town hall meeting led by a senior executive whose laid-back style was completely inappropriate for the occasion. He had taken his jacket off, and was leaning against the podium with one arm draped over it. He frequently turned to look at his slides, but even when he faced his audience, he didn't really look at them because he was slightly hunched over. He wanted to come across as accessible, but instead he came across as indifferent. He put forth little energy and inspired no one.

When you stand, let others see that you are sure of yourself and ready to engage the issues at hand. The best stance is an upright posture that balances firmness with flexibility.

- Plant your feet solidly on the ground, about shoulder-width apart.

- Distribute your weight evenly between your two feet.

- Avoid swaying or rocking.

- Keep your knees unlocked and flexible.

- Relax your hip joints.

- Make sure your shoulders are dropped and relaxed.

- Bring your elbows in a few inches from your sides to give your lungs breathing room.

- Hold your head upright, rather than tilting it forward or cocking it to one side.

If you feel too short at the podium, stand on a small stool. No one will see it, and it will make you appear tall (and more confident).

Where you stand is as important as whether you stand. To take control of a room, take a strong position. Often this is directly in front of the audience—on stage or in a boardroom. Make this your "home base" where you do most of your speaking. Don't pace. Pacing will distract an audience and make you look nervous and unsure of yourself. If you want to move, do so every once in a while. The best time to move is at key junctures in your speech. And if the opportunity presents itself, you can even move forward *into* the audience. Jeffrey Immelt did this when addressing a leadership forum. Instead of reading a speech, he asked the audience what they wanted to know about, then walked right up the steps into the audience and talked to them.[2] It shows boldness that he was willing to step outside his "territory" and meet the audience on theirs.

When Sitting

Stature is equally important when you are sitting in a meeting. Sit tall to project leadership. Not many people do this effectively. Some people sit up, but in a way that is rigid or uncomfortably formal. Others lean forward in a posture that's aggressive and intimidating, as though they're about to pounce on any mistake or slip-up. Others lean back in an overly casual way, as if to say, "I'm here but I'm not really listening." Still others slouch, with a rumpled look of someone who is not really there.

To convey a leadership presence when sitting, follow these guidelines.

- Sit in your whole chair, rather than to one side.

- Sit tall. Don't lean back or lean forward from your waist.

- Sit slightly forward on your chair and put both feet on the ground. If your feet don't reach the floor, adjust the seat you're using or choose a different one.

- If you're wearing a skirt, hold your knees together lightly, but don't jam them together. In pants, you can release your knees more, about hip-width apart.

- Feel your "sit bones" at the bottom of your pelvis. Feel them pressed into the seat of the chair, and make sure your weight is evenly distributed over them.

- Keep your head balanced on top of your spine, not cocked to one side or the other.

- Finally, remove any clutter in front of you, such as water bottles, purses, binders, and cases for glasses. They can be distracting and create an unpolished look. All you need are your notes if you're speaking, or a clean pad for note taking.

Where you sit is as important as how you sit. Sitting at the head of the table, if you are in charge, is acceptable and proper, although some find it "old school." You can show that you're willing to change old hierarchies and are open to new ideas by sitting on the side of the boardroom table. The best place is in the middle (as opposed to the end of the side). Or, you can buy a round table, as the CEO of a mining company we work with did. That shape creates openness and allows everyone to see each other. It's worth the investment!

Whether standing or sitting, your physical stance should be upright and open. In deciding whether to sit or stand, keep in mind that standing always gives you more stature—literally. You will have more power and visibility if you stand. Your voice will be stronger, too. So when you are speaking on a conference call and you want to have greater impact, stand up. Those at the other end of the phone won't see you, but they will hear the difference. And if you choose to sit during a conference call, sit tall. Again, your audience will hear that stature in your voice.

Gestures of a Leader

Your gestures say a lot about you as a leader. The best gestures reflect qualities leaders aspire to: authenticity, openness, strength, and expressiveness. Let's look at how you can embody these qualities when you gesture.

Authentic Gestures

Your gestures should be real and authentic. When working with our clients, we often hear them say: "I'm Italian," or "I'm South Asian," or "I'm Mexican," adding, "I use my hands too much." Yet we rarely feel this is the case. All leaders have their own sense of physicality.

Good speaking is a physical activity: our arms and hands *want* to get involved.

To avoid stiff or excessive gestures, become more conscious of how you normally gesture. Free up that natural energy for gesturing. Gestures will be authentic if you let your body respond to the energy of your words and ideas. If you are at the podium, don't hold on to that piece of furniture for dear life—it will inhibit your natural impulse to gesture. And if you are speaking in front of a boardroom table or at a meeting table, simply strive for gestures that reflect the natural energy you have and the energy you feel at the moment of speaking.

Open Gestures

Good leaders are open with others. Your gestures should reflect this same openness. Many leaders have trouble keeping themselves physically open to their audience. They fold their arms across their chest, knit their hands together, and cross their legs. They make their arms into armor, and come across as closed-minded or defensive.

I once watched several executives of a large natural resource company as they sat on the stage in front of hundreds of shareholders at the annual general meeting. All three executives—the CEO, the CFO, and the head of investor relations—sat there with their hands tightly folded. It had been a challenging year for the company, and the executives were responding to some tough questions. But the signals conveyed by their closed body language only added to the tension in the room. When I later asked why they were doing that, they said a media-relations expert had told them to fold their hands, lest they start gesturing too much. Unfortunately they looked like they were praying—not sending the best message after what had been a difficult year!

Keep your arms and hands open and relaxed. If you are standing, keep your arms loose at your sides so they are free to gesture. You can tuck one arm slightly behind you or put it in your pocket to avoid flailing away with both arms. Every once in a while you can put your hands in both pockets (if you don't have any coins in your pockets) or rest one or both hands on your hips. But keeping both hands loose at your sides will enable you to gesture freely whenever you want to. If you are at the podium, you can keep your arms loosely at your sides, or gently hold the podium. They will be positioned to gesture easily when the time comes. If you are sitting at a table, keep your arms and hands on the table (rather than having them hidden), and they will be ready to gesture. A final word of caution: even when you are listening, remember not to fold your arms or hands. An audience member with such closed body language looks detached and hard to reach.

Strong Gestures

Strong gestures show your commitment to your ideas and to your audience. How should you gesture to convey such strong leadership? Here are guidelines to follow whether you're standing or sitting.

- Gesture from the shoulder. Allow some space between your arms and your sides to ensure that the gesture comes from the entire arm, not just the forearm or wrist.
- Avoid "flipper" gestures from the elbow. Some speakers lock their elbows into their body, and their arms look like flippers, frantically moving and distracting the audience.
- Avoid small wrist gestures, which are weak and seem dismissive.

- Make sure your gestures move in the direction of your audience. Think of them as reaching out to the audience.

- Don't hold a pen or pencil in your hand—it will distract.

- Never point or shake your finger at your audience, this gesture does not become a leader. In the same way—don't make a fist as a gesture.

- Resist the temptation to fix your hair, touch your face, scratch, or fiddle with clothes and jewelry. These grooming or self-preening gestures distract from your leadership image.

Expressive Gestures

Gestures should also be purposeful—they should express your ideas. When you are speaking, think about the importance of the ideas you are delivering, and your desire to persuade your audience. If you are genuinely engaged by what you are saying, you'll naturally suit the action to the word. Brazilian President Dilma Rousseff, while concluding her Oath Ceremony Speech, stood behind the podium and raised both arms so high and wide that she seemed to embrace the entire nation.[3] That said it all!

Then there are occasions when you can do something even more dramatically expressive. Craig Barrett, former chairman of Intel, began his address to an industry conference by getting down on his knees in front of more than 6,000 technology managers, and begging their forgiveness. "We ate crow," Barrett told his audience as he cupped his hands, and knelt his six-foot-three frame before his clients. He then proceeded to elaborate the management missteps that he and his team had made, resulting in the scrapping or delaying of five projects. This was certainly a memorable gesture from the head of a major corporation, and one that visually showed that Intel bowed to its customers.[4]

Finally, be aware of the power of stillness. Actor Peter Ustinov once said: "The secret of acting is to reduce everything to absolute stillness because that gives the map scale. If you are absolutely still, when you move it registers; if you move the whole time, nothing registers."[5] Sometimes stillness, like a pause when you're speaking, can add great emphasis to your point. In fact, when you are not gesturing, think of stillness as your default position. That way you will eliminate any nervous "tics" or energy leaks.

The Face of a Leader

Facial expressions are also critical in conveying the presence of a leader. Our faces are open books that, whatever our words, reveal our state of mind. Author Malcolm Gladwell points out that "All of us, a thousand times a day, read faces . . . We easily parse complex distinctions in facial expression . . . The face is such an extraordinarily efficient instrument of communication."[6]

What can you do to achieve the facial expressions of a leader? Begin by showing that you value your listeners and the act of speaking. If your audience thinks you don't want to speak to them, they won't want to listen to you. Facial animation should also demonstrate your passion and conviction. Let your face get into the act! You can do this by smiling. I do not mean putting on a wide or pasted-on smile. I mean finding within yourself an "inner smile"—a smile that radiates from your feelings about what you are saying.

Just make sure your smiles are appropriate. A false smile is worse than no smile at all. One of our coaches worked with a client who was the spokesperson for a public utility. When coaching him, she noticed that he always smiled! He had a friendly face and his smile certainly warmed his audience. But his smile did not suit most of his messages, since he often conveyed bad news about rate increases or service outages. To correct this habit, our coach asked him to connect emotionally to what he was saying. By doing so he was able to evoke a facial expression that was much more congruent with his words. Our coach encouraged the client to practice in front of a mirror. That way he could see for himself when his expressions reinforced or conflicted with his message.

All the aspects of body language discussed in this chapter—stance, gestures, and facial expressions—are critical to a leader's presence. Practice them, and you will not only "suit the action to the word," you will strengthen your leadership presence.

CHAPTER 26

FIND YOUR LEADER'S VOICE

A voice is an elaborate instrument, which one can use without knowing much about it. But to make sense with it, you really need to know its limits and capabilities.[1]

—Diane Ackerman, *A Natural History of the Senses*

Leaders know how to use their voices. When they take the stage, they project vocal energy that compels the audience to listen. They speak loudly and distinctly, because they know if an audience has to struggle to hear or understand them, their leadership will be compromised. They speak with expression and great vocal range, because they know that if they bore their audience, their leadership will be undermined. A good voice is a leadership imperative. To speak as a leader, you must develop your voice's full capabilities.

Importance of the Voice in Today's Organizations

The voice has always been an important leadership instrument, but never more so than today. Leaders throughout history have developed their voices so they could project a dynamic presence. Cicero, the Roman philosopher and statesman, had a weak voice, which would go to the higher registers when he got passionate. But he improved his voice by studying the famous actors of his day.[2] British prime minister Margaret Thatcher received coaching on "how to project the voice without shrieking." She worked with a voice coach and even met with actor Sir Laurence Olivier "to see whether he had any tips which might be useful."[3]

Most leaders do not work on their voices with this level of dedication. But developing an effective voice has become ever more important today because of the growth of global organizations and new forms of communication. In today's world we need to speak clearly, loudly, and forcefully.

We need to speak *clearly* because business has become more international and every speaker, regardless of their accent or first language, must be understood by a global audience.

We need to speak *loudly* to ensure that everyone hears us whether we are addressing a large audience, speaking on the phone, or involved in a webcast.

We need to speak *forcefully* so that even people who can't see the expression on our faces will not push the mute button or text while we talk.

Today more than ever our voices must be instruments of leadership.

Six Steps to Unlocking the Power of Your Voice

How can you develop the voice of a leader? Here are six steps.

1. Seize the Opportunity to Speak

Don't be content to stand in the wings or sit silently at a meeting. If you want to have the voice of a leader, assume your rightful role in the discussion. Don't wait for someone to call on you. Speak up when you have something to contribute. A leader should be listening to the discussion and asking himself or herself at every turn, "How can I move this conversation forward?" This doesn't mean hogging the stage or talking to hear your own voice. Speaking should always have a higher purpose. Speaking up also means expressing your views even when you feel others may not agree with you. This is the quality of courage discussed in chapter 5. Finally, speaking up means seizing opportunities. Put forward your name as a speaker—for town halls, local events, association meetings, industry conferences, and executive presentations. If you choose to speak up, your voice will become stronger, you will be heard, and you will become a more credible leader.

2. Breathe Freely

Your voice is a wind instrument that's fueled by your breath. You need space in your body so breath can fill you up. The important thing is to be relaxed. If you're tense—either from performance jitters or an accumulation of stress—you can only take in little sips of breath. If your voice gets croaky or hoarse while you're speaking, you may not be breathing enough to support your sound, not supplying your voice with enough fuel. A lack of breath can also affect your ability to think clearly. We've heard clients say that they can't think sometimes when they're presenting—their minds go blank. It's likely they're breathing barely enough to stay upright and there's little oxygen for their brains.

How do we encourage free breath? Try this exercise. Take in a breath, but take it high up in your chest and hold in your stomach muscles. Keep holding in your stomach muscles. Register how that feels. Keep holding them in. Now let out a big sigh and soften all around your stomach region. Allow breath to fill you up from the bottom of your belly to the top of your chest. This exercise will let you experience what a relaxed, generous breath feels like.

Begin to notice your breath. Notice when your breathing is slower and deeper. See which people or situations allow that to happen. Learn to appreciate free breath and how comfortable it allows you to feel in your body. Put notations on your script to remind yourself to breathe. Practice ushering in as much breath as you can and as often as you can. Give your voice and mind a plentiful and dependable supply of oxygen. Then, and only then, will you be able to develop the vocal power necessary to project confident leadership.

Let's say you are in front of an audience, waiting for your turn to speak, and you get increasingly anxious. Try one of the following exercises to restore the flow of breath:

> **Exercise:** Imagine that you're taking in a smell that you love. It could be the smell of someone's perfume or it could be the smell of a flower. Practice using that as a shortcut to trigger relaxation.

> **Exercise:** Notice your mind-set. If your mind is saying "I'm so nervous, I'm so nervous," replace that thought with "Yes, I'm nervous, but I'm going to allow myself to feel what I'm feeling and then fill my body to capacity with breath, and then I'll be able to think."

Breath is essential to speaking as a leader. The word "inspire" comes from the Latin word *inspirare*, meaning "in" plus "to breathe." When you breathe in, you have the capacity to inspire others. You will be unlocking the potential of your voice.

3. Turn Up the Volume

Today's "cubicle culture" and open office environments have encouraged us to grow quieter and quieter as the workplace walls come down. You might spend hours at your desk keeping your voice down so as not to disturb those around you. Then when you go into a boardroom or take part in a conference call, you may still be using your "quiet" voice. Adjust your volume to suit your space and technology. When you do speak up, take a deep breath and truly speak up. Make your voice resonate with authority. We all have great vocal equipment, but we need to use it. Your lungs and vocal cords get a good workout when you call out to a friend on the street to get his or her attention, or cheer at a sports event, or hail a cab. You may be thinking that's just shouting. But if you expect people to sit up and listen to you at a meeting, you must commit fully to having your ideas heard. That commitment will create strength and depth for your voice, and you will be seen and heard as a leader who really commands attention.

In our workshops we show leaders how to unlock the power of their voices by speaking loudly enough that everyone in the room can hear comfortably. Invariably they ask, "Aren't I too loud?" That's because they're unused to hearing themselves so well. I'll never forget one woman who said, "But I've been told I'm too loud." Our instructor asked who had told her such a thing. She thought back—way back—and remembered that it was her two little brothers who admonished her for being too loud when she looked after them. They were from a culture that traditionally did not encourage women to speak up. Twenty years later she's still taking directions from her little brothers because she formed a vocal habit of always speaking quietly—not a useful habit in the corporate world. Some women find it uncomfortable, even frightening, to hear and feel the power of their own voice, and so they soften their voice and dilute their power.

Men, too, sometimes speak in softer tones than is required. A male client came to us because he felt his voice was too soft. The first thing he said when he met our voice coach was: "I have a very quiet voice. It runs in our family. My mother actually spoke very loudly and my father didn't. Now my two sons have very soft voices." And to give the whole scenario a reason for being, he said, "It's genetic." His decision to come to us to strengthen his voice was a very good thing. Our coaching will enable him to break the pattern and become a better role model for his sons. What about people who deliberately soften their voices so that their audience will have to come to them? It's manipulative! You should make it easy for your audience to hear you.

As a leader you must claim your voice, claim your right to speak with power by turning up the volume. Commit to that full sound from the beginning of a sentence all the way to the end. Many people start each sentence with appropriate volume and then halfway through lose confidence or begin thinking of their next thought, and trail off. So the audience hears the idea fall away. An audience could take this as an indication that the speaker isn't committed to the talk, and use the opportunity to tune out. Instead of letting this happen, *hold your ground vocally.* Don't let your mind rush ahead to the next thought (with the result that your voice falls off). Stay focused on what you are saying. And pause between your sentences to think ahead to the next thought.

To develop the habit of turning up your volume, warm up your voice daily. Singing in the shower works really well: the hot water relaxes you and the acoustics are great. Sing along in your car with your favorite artists and get used to the sound and feeling of vocal vibrations. And when you are speaking, strive for a volume that allows everyone in the room or on the conference call to hear and understand every word you are delivering.

4. Use All Your Notes

You were born with a voice capable of two and a half octaves (20 keys on the piano). That range allows you to sound brilliantly expressive. But the range can get severely diminished unless we practice using all our notes. An audience at a meeting gets quickly bored when someone speaks with a limited range. The speaker becomes monotone and there's not enough variation to keep the audience's interest. Men and women have different issues when it comes to using their full range. Women's voices frequently get caught in the higher registers, through tension or habit. When they speak this way they lose their authoritative tone. Some women feel the higher notes make them sound cheerful and obliging, but that's a very limiting profile. If you always sound cheerful and obliging, how will an audience recognize your strength and capacity to lead?

Men, in contrast, are more likely to get trapped in the lower registers of their voices. They may tuck their chin in and push their larynx down in an attempt to sound manly. This limits the voice to just the chest and throat resonators, thus ironing out any color or variation. Drain out the color and variation in your voice, and you'll lose your audience. Compare that monotone to the more colorful one a man might use when he's out with his friends, or reading to his children.

The voice's color is also lost when we get caught up in repeated vocal patterns. One we hear frequently in The Humphrey Group's work is "upspeak," the habit of lifting the voice up at the end of a thought, which sounds like you're asking a question rather than making an assertion. It makes an individual sound unsure. Stay grounded through the full sentence. Don't leave your messages dangling up there as if you're asking, "Is this okay?"

Don't get stuck in just a few notes or play the same tune over and over. Use all your notes and vary your melodies. People will be happy to listen to you.

5. Find Your Authentic Voice

Often people, who in everyday conversation are relaxed, funny, charming, and tuned in to their authentic selves, resort to a dull, lifeless voice when they are "on stage." Sometimes a client will say, "I'm only talking numbers. It's really boring." That's even more reason to make those numbers compelling with your authentic voice. Sometimes clients' voices will recede because they're using PowerPoint and they're thinking of themselves as narrators rather than speakers. The same flat tones can characterize the voice mail individuals leave. Stop to consider that this may be the first exposure someone has to you. If you want them to hear that you're smart, warm, and approachable, then practice finding those authentic qualities in your voice.

Authenticity not only involves using a natural tone, it also demands a conversational pace. Such a pace allows us breathing time and gives our audience a moment to think. The most persuasive leaders talk at the same speed as a good conversation—not too fast and not too slow. They have a pace that allows every word to be heard clearly. And they pause between their ideas, giving their audience time to reflect on what they've said and giving themselves time to think ahead to the next idea. Using your authentic voice shows that you are determined and excited about an idea. When someone speaks in a way that's real, it's easier for the audience to follow them and get excited about what they're saying.

6. Articulate Clearly

We all speak thousands of words every day, but we do not sound like leaders unless we put commitment and energy into forming those words. If you don't articulate precisely, listeners may be left scratching their heads. Everyone has an accent. We would find it dull if everyone spoke English the same way. The issue here is not accent: it's clarity.

What can you do to articulate more clearly? You have to bring muscularity to the formation of your words. The next time you're in a crowded room, give your lips a good workout so you can be heard above the din. Commit to articulation. If you bring that same energy to a presentation or a conference call, you will not only sound more forceful, but you'll feel that way, too. For daily practice, try these exercises.

> **Exercise:** Recall the tongue twisters you knew when you were growing up. Now is the time to revive them and practice them daily. And it doesn't matter what language they're in—they're brilliant exercises for your articulating muscles.

Exercise: Practice talking with the cork from a wine bottle in your mouth. Hold the cork between your teeth and practice speaking a few lines from a text. Then recite the passage again without the cork. You will find your mouth is open wider and your articulation is much stronger.

And if you want proof that an open mouth is necessary for good articulation, watch the great performers when they sing. Watch Mick Jagger, for example. He really opens his mouth WIDE!

As you've seen in this brief excursion through the voice, we have tremendous vocal powers. You can develop your voice as a powerful leadership tool with these new habits. Speak up, breathe freely, turn up the volume, use your complete register, be authentic, and articulate fully. There's an expression that we like to use in The Humphrey Group: love the sound of your own voice. If you do, your voice will develop into one of the best instruments for leadership that you have.

CONCLUSION

ALWAYS LEADING, ALWAYS INFLUENCING

This book that you have just read might have been called *Always Leading*. It has emphasized the importance of seeing every speaking situation as a leadership moment. I know you will take away more than a few tips for speaking well. You will derive from this book an understanding that wherever you are, whatever the occasion, whomever you are talking to, you have a *leadership opportunity*. My call to action to you is that you internalize the following mission:

I will work to influence and inspire every audience—large or small.

To achieve this goal you'll want to master the four broad steps outlined in this book. Develop a leader's mind-set, script yourself as a leader, use the language of leadership, and achieve a leader's presence. But that is only the beginning.

Large and Small Stages

Every day you have dozens of opportunities to make believers out of your colleagues, your peers, and your staff. You are always on stage. Every talk, presentation, e-mail, and voice mail is a chance to lead. It's an opportunity to persuade and inspire your audience. Too often people think that leadership is played out only on grand, public stages. It's not. It must also be played out when we're in conversation, on the phone, in meetings, and in elevators. Otherwise, we'll miss these frequent opportunities to lead every day, every hour, every moment. In fact, increasingly your biggest leadership opportunities may well come on these small stages.

The Mike Is Always On

Remember that the microphone is always on. There are many situations where leaders feel they are offstage, but they aren't. Look around. You have an audience whenever people are present. These "stages" can be offices, restaurants, and golf courses. In these situations we may feel we can take off our leadership mantle and say whatever we want. But for a leader there is never an offstage role.

Even a speaker as impressive as former United States president Ronald Reagan had moments when he forgot that the mike is always on. He once joked behind a radio microphone he didn't know was on, "My fellow Americans, I am pleased to tell you that I've signed legislation that will outlaw Russia forever. We begin bombing in five minutes."[1] This celebrated display of "off-mike mentality" may be an extreme case, but we do see public figures today tarnishing their reputation with inappropriate personal tweets. Executives and other people in guiding roles frequently make the mistake of thinking there can be downtime for a leader.

Larry Page, CEO of Google, read a 394-word statement with a lack of enthusiasm in his first conference call with analysts. The result? The next day the company lost $15 billion in market value. He learned that the mike is always on and, recently, in his second conference call to analysts, he "wowed investors, driving the stock price up by 12 percent."[2] Every speech, every analyst call is an opportunity to lead and inspire.

Even "chit chat" is a leadership opportunity. I recently met a new client, who said she often says the wrong thing in business small talk events. To illustrate, she told me that she was at a conference, and saw a member of her firm's board of directors. She told me she didn't know what to say, so she blurted out, "you look tired. Have you been travelling?" The executive was taken aback, but graciously said: "Why yes, I have just returned from China." Will he remember her for her board presentations, which had gone well, or for this comment that came too quickly because she didn't realize the mike is always on?

Just think of all those situations when you may not have been as prepared as you wished, when you did not speak up at an important juncture in a meeting, or when you spoke up but said the wrong thing or something that forced you to do damage control. Those are lost leadership opportunities.

Every Situation Is a Leadership Moment

Recognize every situation as an opportunity to lead and inspire others with your convictions. While this reality puts pressure on you, it also will energize you. It gives you a reason for being strong, keeping positive, and staying on message.

Every audience you speak to wants to be led by you. Every audience wants to believe in you. Speaking well is one of the greatest leadership opportunities you have. As Cicero, the famous Roman statesman, wrote more than two thousand years ago:

> *The one point in which we have our very greatest advantage over the brute creation is that we hold converse one with another, and can reproduce our thoughts in word. Who therefore would not rightly admire this faculty, and deem it his [and her] duty to exert himself to the utmost in this field?*[3]

Speaking well allows you to move people with the power of your thinking. It allows you to inspire others to pursue paths they hadn't considered before. The power of speech is yours. Not just the power to utter words, but the power to influence others with those words.

To achieve that power, take this book as your guide. These techniques you have learned in *Speaking as a Leader* will serve you well, whether you are an aspiring leader or one who has reached the heights of your profession or organization.

I also recommend that you study the great speakers of classical and modern times. You'd be amazed how remarkably current is the advice in Aristotle's *Rhetoric*, Cicero's *On the Orator*, and Quintilian's *Institutes of Oratory*. And take a look at Plutarch's *Life of Demosthenes*. It is the story of a man who worked his entire life to perfect his speaking, and who became known as the greatest orator of classical times.

For the study of modern speeches, a good starting point is the collection in William Safire's *Lend Me Your Ears: Great Speeches in History*. As Theodore C. Sorensen, John F. Kennedy's speechwriter and biographer, explained, what made a great speech in 1940 or 1961 is not much different from what makes a great speech today. He summarized some of those key qualities: "Speaking from the heart, to the heart, directly, not too complicated, relatively brief sentences, words that are clear to everyone."[4]

Finally, keep this in mind: you have it within you to be great. Just remember that every time you speak, you can make believers out of your listeners. This is not a sidebar to your leadership. It is the very essence of your leadership. If you want to lead, accept this role. Seize this opportunity whenever you can. Realize that you have the power to create believers. Make *Speaking as a Leader* more than a book on your shelf. Make it a way of life that will enrich the lives of others.

ENDNOTES

Introduction

1. Jack Welch, "25 Lessons from Jack Welch," http://www.1000ventures. com/business_guide/mgmt_new-model_25lessons-welch.html/.
2. Noel Tichy, *The Leadership Engine*, (New York: HarperCollins Publishers, 2002), 101-102. For a fuller treatment of the subject, see chapter 5: "The Heart of Leadership: It Starts with Ideas."

Chapter 1

1. Lewis Carroll, *Alice's Adventures in Wonderland* and *Through the Looking-Glass* (Toronto: Penguin Books, 2009), chapter 6, p. 56.
2. Sergey Brin, interview by Yair Lapid, Ulpan Shishi (Studio Friday), Channel 2, (Israel). YouTube video, 2007. http://www.youtube.com/watch?v=zlx5FOvbj84.
3. Mark Zuckerberg, interview at D: All Things Digital conference, "D8," June 2, 2010, video clip, http://d8.allthingsd.com/?s=Mark+Zuckerberg.

ENDNOTES

4. Kinross Gold Corporation, http://www.Kinrossgold.com.
5. Agrium, http://www.agrium.com/sustainability/our_approach.jsp.
6. Michael Dell, *Direct from Dell*, (New York: HarperBusiness, 1999), p. 108.

Chapter 2

1. Anton Pavlovich Checkhov, "Fat and Thin," in *The Tales of Checkhov Volume 13: Love and Other Stories*, (Middlesex, UK: The Echo Library, 2006), pp. 102–121.
2. Duff McDonald, "Can This Man Make Morgan Stanley Great Again?" *Fortune*, April 11, 2011, p. 108.
3. Peter Elkind and David Whitford, "An Accident Waiting to Happen," *Fortune*, February 7, 2011, p. 129.
4. CNN Wire Staff, "BP apology campaign begins airing," CNN U.S., http://articles.cnn.com/2010-06-02/us/oil.spill.bp.apology_1_tony-hayward-spill-gulf-of-mexico-oil/.
5. Adam Bryant, "The Quest to Build a Better Boss," *New York Times*, March 13, 2011, BU1, BU7.

Chapter 3

1. Garry Wills, *Lincoln at Gettysburg*, (New York: Simon and Schuster, 1992), p. 37.
2. GSM (Global System for Mobile Communications), TDMA (Time Division Multiple Access), and CDMA (Code Division Multiple Access). All refer to approaches to sending messages within cell phone networks.
3. John Bartlett, ed., *Familiar Quotations*, (Toronto: Little, Brown and Company, 1992), 158. The original quotation from Francis Bacon is: *Nam et ipsa scientia potestas est* from "De Haeresibus" [Of Heresies] in his *Meditationes Sacrae* [Sacred Meditations] (1597).

ENDNOTES

Chapter 4

1. Sir Winston Churchill, from his speech at the Lord Mayor's banquet in London, November 9, 1954, quoted in Winston S. Churchill, *Never Give In! The Best of Winston Churchill's Speeches*, (New York: Hyperion, 2003), p. 488.
2. Quoted in Joe Nick Patoski, *Willie Nelson: An Epic Life* (New York: Hachette Digital, 2008.
3. William Safire, ed., *Lend Me Your Ears: Great Speeches in History*, (New York: W.W. Norton & Company, 1997), pp. 399–400.
4. BP, *Summary Review 2010*, "A letter from Carl-Henric Svanberg, Chairman," March 2, 2011, http://www.bp.com/summaryreview.
5. Voltaire, *Candide, ou l'Optimisme* [Candide: or, All for the Best] first published in 1759.

Chapter 5

1. Jonathan Daniels, press secretary to Harry S. Truman, quoted in Kathleen Hall Jamieson, *Eloquence in an Electronic Age*, (New York: Oxford University Press, 1988), p. 173.
2. Loïck Roche and John Sadowsky, "Stories and Storytelling: An Example of Best Practices of Leadership in a High-Tech Environment," *Business Leadership Review* 1:111, October 2004.
3. Steve Jobs, commencement address delivered June 12, 2005. Prepared text published in the *Stanford Report*, June 14, 2005, http://news.stanford .edu/news/2005/june15/jobs-061505.html.
4. Jonathan Storm, "The billion-dollar maverick," *The Sunday Star* (Toronto), September 21, 1997.
5. Michael Dell, *Direct from Dell* (New York: HarperBusiness, 1999), p. 111.

Chapter 6

1. The author attended a dinner during which Newton discussed "the actor" and spoke these words about how the actor listens

2. Ernest Hemingway, from a letter of advice to a young writer, reported in Malcolm Cowley, "Mister Papa," *LIFE* magazine, January 10, 1949, Volume 26, No. 2, p. 90.
3. Aaron Scott, "Letters in response to the 12.5.10 Issue," *The New York Times Magazine*, December 19, 2010, MM10.
4. Helen Keller, *The Story of My Life*, (Mineola, New York: Dover Large Print Classics, 2002), p. 156.
5. Drew Gilpin Faust, "Leadership without a Secret Code," Corner Office, *The New York Times*, November 1, 2009, p. 2.

Chapter 7

1. James C. Humes, *The Sir Winston Method* (New York: William Morrow and Company Inc., 1991), p. 19.
2. Exodus 4:10.
3. Acts 7:22.
4. Kathleen Hall Jamieson, *Eloquence in an Electronic Age*, (New York: Oxford University Press, 1988), 3. Hall draws these observations about Demosthenes from Plutarch, *Lives of the Noble Greeks*, ed. Edmund Fuller, (New York: Dell, 1959), pp. 354–356.
5. Stephen B. Oates, *With Malice toward None: A Life of Abraham Lincoln*, (New York: Harper & Row, 1977), p. 20.
6. Elizabeth Drew, *On the Edge: The Clinton Presidency*, (New York: Simon & Schuster, 1994), pp. 77–78.
7. Carmine Gallo, *The Presentation Secrets of Steve Jobs*, (New York: McGraw Hill, 2010), pp. 182–184.

Chapter 8

1. Carroll, *Alice's Adventures in Wonderland and Through the Looking-Glass*, chapter 4, p. 161.

Chapter 9

1. This Henry Ward Beecher story can be found in various sources, including: Earl Prevette, *How to Turn Your Ability into Cash*, (Philadelphia: Mark Parshall, 1953) and Richard Carman Borden, *Public Speaking—As Listeners Like it!*, (New York: Harper & Brothers Publishers, 1938).
2. Benazir Bhutto, "Speech on Islam," Kiev, Ukraine, April 26, 2007, http://www.ppp.org.pk/mbb/speeches.
3. Morgan Freeman, 77th Academy Awards, February 27, 2005.
4. Winston Churchill, quoted in Ted Goodman, *The Forbes Book of Business Quotations*, (New York: Black Dog & Leventhal Publishers, 1997), p. 317.
5. Stephen Hawking, "Science in the Next Millennium" (lecture presented at the Second Millennium Evening at The White House, March 6, 1998).
6. Horace, *Epistles* 1.2.40, quoted in John Bartlett, ed., *Familiar Quotations* (Toronto: Little, Brown and Company, 1992), p. 97.

Chapter 10

1. This anecdote was told to me by someone in the audience.

Chapter 11

1. Kenneth Grahame, Seth Lerer, ed., *The Wind in the Willows: An Annotated Edition*, (Boston: Harvard University Press, 2009), p. 254.
2. John Heilemann and Mark Halperin, *Game Change*, (New York: Harper Perennial, 2010), p. 110.
3. Eisenhower quoted in James C. Humes, *The Sir Winston Method: the Five Secrets of Speaking the Language of Leadership*, (New York: William Morrow and Company, Inc., 1991), 46.
4. Churchill quoted in Humes, *The Sir Winston Method: the Five Secrets of Speaking the Language of Leadership*, p. 46.
5. Aristotle, "Poetics," Chapter 8. From Introduction to Aristotle, ed. Richard McKeon, (New York: McGraw-Hill, Inc., 1947), p. 635.

6. Larry Page, quoted in Brendan Coffey, "Meet More Billionaires Who Tweet: Brin, Kholsa, Pickens & More," *Forbes* (online), April 13, 2011.
7. Bill Gates, Twitter, June 20, 2011.

Chapter 12

1. Carroll, *Alice's Adventures in Wonderland* and *Through the Looking-Glass*, chapter 12, p. 105.
2. Aristotle, *Poetics* 1450b26.
3. Churchill quoted in James C. Humes, *The Sir Winston Method*, 114.
4. Jeffrey R. Immelt, Chairman and CEO, GE, Commencement Address at Dartmouth College, June 2004, The Humphrey Group Archives.
5. Adapted from Bill Clinton's inaugural address, January 20, 1993. Quoted in The Office of the Federal Register, *Public Papers of the Presidents of the United States*, (Washington: Government Printing Office, 1994), p. 1.

Chapter 13

1. John F. Kennedy, inaugural address, January 20, 1961. Quoted in Halford Ryan, ed., *The Inaugural Addresses of Twentieth-Century American Presidents*, (Westport, CT: Praegar Publishers, 1993) p. 188.
2. See "I am prepared to die" speech at http://www.nelsonmandela.org/index.php/memory.
3. William Safire, p. 210.
4. Ibid., pp. 50–51.
5. See Prince Harry's Tribute to Diana at http:/www.americanrhetoric.com/speeches/princeharrydianaeulogy.htm.
6. Stephen Dyer, Chief Financial Officer, Agrium Inc., remarks at a Leadership Retreat, June 2011.

Chapter 14

1. Carroll, *Alice's Adventures in Wonderland and Through the Looking-Glass*, p. 61.

ENDNOTES

2. Allen R. Myers, "A Voice Finds Itself in Demand," *The New York Times*, April 16, 2000, p. 2.
3. Blaise Pascal, *Lettres Provinciales* [1656–1657], no. 16.
4. Churchill and Sorensen quoted in Peter Appleborne, "Is Eloquence Overrated?" *The New York Times*," January 13, 2008, p. 3.
5. Lou Gehrig "Farewell to Baseball" Speech, quoted in William Safire, pp. 399–400.

Chapter 15

1. Carroll, *Alice's Adventures in Wonderland and Through the Looking-Glass*, p. 132.
2. Paul M. Zall, ed., *Mark Twain Laughing: Humorous Anecdotes by and about Samuel L. Clemens*, (Knoxville: The University of Tennessee Press, 1997), p. 103.
3. Exxon Mobil Corporation, *2010 Summary Annual Report*, p. 3.

Chapter 16

1. Charles Francis, *Wisdom Well Said*, (El Prado, NM: Levine Mesa Press, 2009), p. 474.
2. Ronald Reagan, *Speaking My Mind: Selected Speeches*, (New York: Simon and Schuster, 1989), p. 292.
3. Eric Schmidt quoted in http://ww.msnbc.msn.com/id/41179589.
4. Author's word and syllable count.
5. Theodore Sorensen, *Kennedy*, (New York: Harper & Row, 1965), p. 270.
6. Winston Churchill, speech on receiving the London *Times* Literary Award, November 2, 1949, quoted in Richard Langworth, ed., *Churchill by Himself*, (New York: PublicAffairs, 2011), p. 61.
7. *La Presse*, October 8, 1997, translated for me from the French by the speaker.
8. Lincoln quoted in William Safire, ed., *Lend Me Your Ears*, pp. 823, 828.

ENDNOTES

Chapter 17

1. William Jefferson Clinton's Address on Health Care Reform, September 22, 1993, at http://millercenter.org/scripps/archive/speeches/detail/3926.
2. Louis Gerstner, Chairman's Remarks at IBM Annual Meeting, April 25, 1994. The Humphrey Group Archives.
3. Jeffrey R. Immelt, Chairman and CEO, GE, Commencement Address at Dartmouth College, June 2004. The Humphrey Group Archives.
4. Clara Moskowitz, "NASA Launches Space Shuttle Endeavour on Final Voyage," May 16, 2011, http://www.space.com/11677-nasa-shuttle-launch-endeavour-final-mission-sts-134-liftoff.html.

Chapter 18

1. Hillary Clinton, Concession Speech (Address ending her presidential campaign given to supporters), *New York Times Online*, June 7, 2008.
2. Steve Jobs, former CEO, Apple Inc., Macworld 2007 Speech introducing the iPhone. At http://www.engadget.com/2007/01/09/live-from-macworld-2007-steve-jobs-keynote.
3. William Safire, ed., *Lend Me Your Ears*, p. 894.
4. Arthur Quinn, *Figures of Speech: 60 Ways To Turn a Phrase*, (Salt Lake City, Utah: Peregrine Smith Books, 1982), pp. 93–95.
5. Quintilian, *Institutes of Oratory*, 9.1.21.
6. Aristotle, *Rhetoric*, trans. by W. Rhys Roberts (New York: Modern Library, 1954). Book III, chapter 11.
7. Ursula Burns quoted in Adam Bryant, "Xerox's New Chief Tries to Redefine Its Culture," *The New York Times*, Business Section, February 20, 2010.
8. William J. Clinton: Press Briefing by Mike McCurry, January 30, 1998. At http://www.presidency.ucsb.edu/ws/index.php?pid=48187.
9. Indra Nooyi quoted in Betsy Morris, "The Pepsi Challenge: Can This Snack and Soda Giant Go Healthy? CEO Indra Nooyi Says Yes, But Cola Wars and Corn Prices Will Test Her Leadership," *Fortune*, March 3, 2008, p. 58.

10. Bono, commencement address at Harvard University, June 12, 2001, quoted in Ken Gewertz and Alvin Powell, "Rocker Bono to Grads: Rebel against Indifference," *Harvard University Gazette*, June 2001.

11. Eduardo Saverin, "Facebook Co-Founder Speaks Publicly: What I Learned From Watching *The Social Network*," CNBC Guest Blog, October 15, 2010, http://www.cnbc.com/id/39675388.

12. Martin Luther King, Jr., quoted in Drew D. Hansen, *The Dream* (New York: HarperCollins Publishers, 2003), p. 179.

13. Robert Slater, *Jack Welch and the GE Way: Management Insights and Leadership Secrets of the Legendary CEO* (New York: McGraw Hill, 1999), pp. 135–140.

14. Dilma Rousseff, "Oath Ceremony Speech," Official transcript as released by Brazil's Ministry of External Relations, January 4, 2011, http://tortillaconsal.com/tortilla/print/7552.

15. Jeff Bezos, founder and CEO, Amazon.com, Interview in Academy of Achievement, http://www.achievement.org/autodoc/page/bez0int-6.

16. Steve Jobs, Macworld 2007 keynote address, quoted in Carmine Gallo, *Presentation Secrets*, p. 159.

Chapter 19

1. Margaret Thatcher, Speech to Conservative Women's Conference, May 26, 1982, http://www.margaretthatcher.org/document/104948.

Chapter 20

1. Donald Fites, Chairman and CEO, Caterpillar, "Retooling for the New Economy," A Speech to *Business Week CEO Summit*, Washington, D. C., September 24, 1998, reprinted in *The Corporate Report*, No. 26, January 31, 1999, p. 22.

2. CNN, "Ted Turner donates $1 billion to 'U.N. causes,'" September 19, 1997, http://edition.cnn.com/US/9709/18/turner.gift/#1.

ENDNOTES

3. Bill & Melinda Gates Foundation, "Bill and Melinda Gates Announce a $100 Million Gift to Establish the Bill and Melinda Gates Children's Vaccine Program," December 2, 1998, http://www.gatesfoundation.org/press-releases/Pages/accelerating-access-to-new-vaccines-for-children-in-developing-nations-981202.aspx.

4. Bradley Blackburn, "The Giving Pledge: Billionaires Promise to Donate at Least Half Their Fortunes to Charity," ABC World News, August 4, 2010, http://abcnews.go.com/WN/bill-gates-warren-buffett-organize-billionaire-giving-pledge/story?id=11325984.

5. An interview with Mark Zuckerburg from *OUR TIME*, a documentary by The Young Americans Project, http://tyap.com.

6. Garry Wills, *Lincoln at Gettysburg: The Words that Remade America* (New York: Simon & Schuster, 1992), p. 221.

7. Samuel J. Palmisano, IBM chairman and chief executive officer, "Final Remarks," PartnerWorld Leadership Conference 2011, February 15, 2011, http://www.ibm.com/ibm/sjp/02_15_2011.html.

8. Angelina Jolie, World Refugee Day 2009 Address, http://www.sweetspeeches.com/s/1705-angelina-jolie-world-refugee-day-2009-address.

9. John F. Welch, chairman and chief executive officer, General Electric Company, "A Learning Company and its Quest for Six Sigma," April 23, 1998. http://www.callcentres.com.au/GE2_Jack_Welch.htm#Learning%20Company.

Chapter 21

1. Quintilian, *Institutes of Oratory*, Book 6, chapter 3.

2. "Short People Rise Up in Anger at Reich," May 15, 2002, http://www.shortsupport.org/News/0312.html.

3. Mark Twain, "Address at the Royal Literary Fund Banquet," London, May 4, 1900, in *Mark Twain's Speeches*.

4. Stephen Hawking, "Science in the Next Millenium," White House Millenium Council, 2000, http://clinton4.nara.gov/Initiatives/Millennium/evenings.html.

240

Chapter 22

1. Margaret Thatcher, *The Path to Power*, (London: HarperCollins Publishers, 1995), p. 296.
2. Nigel Kennedy, *Always Playing*, (London: Weidenfeld and Nicolson, 1991), p. 24.
3. William Safire, ed., *Lend Me Your Ears*, pp. 111–112.

Chapter 23

1. Carol Gelderman, *All the Presidents' Words*, (New York: Walker and Company, 1997), p. 6.
2. Philip G. Clampitt, Robert J. Dekoch, *Embracing Uncertainty: the Essence of Leadership*, (New York: M.E. Sharpe, Inc., 2001), p. 65.
3. *Casablanca*, directed by Michael Curtiz (1942; Burbank, CA: Warner Bros.).

Chapter 24

1. Ralph Waldo Emerson, *The Prose Works of Ralph Waldo Emerson*, Vol. II, (Boston: J.R. Osgood and Co., 1875), p. 410.
2. Peter Appleborne, "Bill Clinton's Uncertain Journey," *New York Times*, March 8, 1992.
3. Michael Ellsberg, *The Power of Eye Contact: Your Secret for Success in Business, Love, and Life,* (New York: HarperCollins, 2010), p. 1.
4. Diane Ackerman, *A Natural History of the Senses*, (New York: Vintage Books, 1990), p. 230.
5. Ibid., 229.
6. Constantin Stanislavski, *An Actor's Handbook*, (New York: Theatre Arts Books, 1963), p. 61.

Chapter 25

1. Hardin Craig and David Bevington, eds., *The Complete Works of Shakespeare*, (Glenview, Illinois: Scott, Foresman and Company, 1973), p. 921.

2. Told to me by an executive at GE who was there.
3. Dilma Rousseff, Oath Ceremony Speech, http://www.youtube.com/watch?v=lsWOZltZ4VI.
4. Jason Kelly and Ian King, "Playing Catch-up at Intel," *Financial Post* (Canada), October 26, 2004, p. 9.
5. Peter Ustinov, *Quotable Ustinov*, (Toronto: Doubleday Canada Limited, 1995), p. 76.
6. Malcolm Gladwell, "The Naked Face," *The New Yorker*, August 5, 2002.

Chapter 26

1. Diane Ackerman, *A Natural History of The Senses*, (New York: Vintage Books, 1991), p. 193.
2. John Carew Rolfe, *Cicero and his Influence* (New York: Cooper Square Publishers, 1963), p. 67.
3. Margaret Thatcher, The Path to Power (London: HarperCollins Publishers, 1995), p. 295.

Conclusion

1. Ronald Reagan, quoted in "Quotable gaffes by world leaders," *The Ottawa Citizen*, July 11, 1997, taken from David Olive's *Political Babble: The 1,000 Dumbest Things Ever Said by Politicians*, (Toronto: John Wiley and Sons Inc., 1992).
2. Larry Page's transformation as a communicator is described in an article entitled "The New Establishment 2011" in *Vanity Fair*, October 2011, p. 192.
3. Cicero, *De Oratore*, I, 8.33.
4. Theodore C. Sorensen quoted in Peter Applebome's "Is Eloquence Overrated?," *The New York Times*, January 13, 2008, p. 3.

INDEX

INDEX

INDEX

INDEX

INDEX